ADVANTAGE STUDY SKILLS

Produced by Richard John Smith
Director of *'Problem Solving Tutoring Services'* Website at http://www.rjs-tutor.co.uk/

Author of *'At 47'*

Storefront

http://www.lulu.com/spotlight/RJPublications

ADVANTAGE STUDY SKILLS

(A manual designed to assist teachers and students)

By

Richard Smith

www.rjs-tutor.co.uk

Produced by Richard John Smith: rjsleeds@yahoo.co.uk

Director of *'Problem Solving Tutoring Services'*

Copyright ©1994 Richard John Smith

The moral right of the author has been asserted

First Limited Edition 1994

Second Revised Edition 2013

ISBN: 978-1-907910-10-4

Editorial Note

Additional material (edited classroom notes from **1997** until **2004**) was incorporated into **Part 2,** as a direct response to requests made by students during my Teaching Practice (from **October 1997** to **April 1998**). The material had originally been designed as *'handouts'*– which accounts for the variation in style and presentation. The contents relate largely to the Humanities and Social Science fields as these were the areas of my expertise at that time.

Further amendments were made throughout **2012** and **2013** in preparation for this Second Edition. Where the material in **Part 1** has been geared to meet the needs of the general reader that found in **Part 2** is of greater interest to those studying the Humanities or the Social Sciences. The information provided by the sources listed in the **Bibliography** and elsewhere is gratefully acknowledged.

Contents

INTRODUCTION 12

PART 1: STUDY AIDS 13

STUDY AID 1: Note-Taking Skills 15

Section 1: Opening comments 17

Section 2: Reasons for note-taking 18

Section 3: The characteristics of good and bad notes 19

Section 4: Nucleated Notes 20

Section 5: The advantages and disadvantages of nucleated notes 20

Section 6: Sequential Notes 20

Section 7: The advantages and disadvantages of sequential notes 21

Section 8: Abbreviations 22

Section 9: Closing comments 22

Appendix 1: Sample *'contents page'* 23

Appendix 2: The development of nucleated notes 24

Appendix 3: Fifty-Two Standard Abbreviations 25

STUDY AID 2: Revision Skills 27

Section 1: Opening comments 29

Section 2: Types of research 30

Section 3: Memory techniques 30

Section 4: Reasons for failure 31

Section 5: The relationship between subject areas and different learning methods 32

Section 6: Closing comments 32

Appendix 1: The learning process 33

Appendix 2: Two possible rates of learning 33

Appendix 2: Example of a *'Revision Timetable'* 34

STUDY AID 3: Thinking Skills **35**

Section 1: Opening comments 37

Section 2: The Characteristics of effective thinking 38

Section 3: Obstacles to effective thinking 39

Section 4: Symptoms of poor thinking 39

Section 5: Ways to improve thinking 40

Section 6: Handling evidence 41

Section 7: The three parts of an argument 42

Section 8: Developing an argument 43

Section 9: Modifying an argument 43

Section 10: Strengthening an argument 43

Section 11: Closing comments 44

STUDY AID 4: Writing Skills **45**

Section 1: Opening comments 47

Section 2: The characteristics of effective writing 48

Section 3: The differences between the written and spoken word 49

Section 4: The *'golden rules'* to effective writing 49

Section 5: Preparing to write effectively 50

Section 6: Gaining precision when writing 50

Section 7: Things to avoid when writing 51

Section 8: The *'active'* and the *'passive'* voice 52

Section 9: Circumlocutions 52

Section 10: '*Signposting*' 53

Section 11: *'Signpost'* Words 53

Section 12: *'Link'* Words 54

Section 13: Closing comments 55

Appendix 1: A *'communication chain'* and its vulnerability to *'noise'* 56

Appendix 2: The impressions formed by good and bad writing 56

STUDY AID 5: Free Writing 57

Section 1: Opening comments 59

Section 2: Methodology 59

Section 3: Assessment of free-writing 60

Section 4: Advantages of free-writing 60

Section 5: Ways to improve writing style 60

Section 6: Closing comments 61

Appendix 1: The stages of producing a written work 62

STUDY AID 6: Assignment Planning 63

Section 1: Opening comments 65

Section 2: Types of assignments 66

Section 3: Types of essay 67

Section 4: The purpose of assignments 67

Section 5: Subject selection 67

Section 6: Title selection 68

Section 7: Planning an assignment 68

Section 8: Completed planning notes 70

Section 9: Readership 70

Section 10: Levels of readership 70

Section 11: Essay and report writing 71

Section 12: Stages in report writing 71

Section 13: Plagiarism 72

Section 14: Closing comments 72

STUDY AID 7: Introductions **73**

Section 1: Opening comments 75

Section 2: Types of Introduction 75

Section 3: Effective Introductions 76

Section 4: Ways to kill a good Introduction 76

Section 5: Introducing arguments 77

Section 6: Closing comments 77

STUDY AID 8: Arguing Skills **79**

Section 1: Opening comments 81

Section 2: Essay conventions 81

Section 3: Prioritisation 82

Section 4: Effective argumentation 83

Section 5: Characteristics of a good argument 83

Section 6: Closing an argument 84

Section 7: Grouping causes 84

Section 8: The advantages of causal groupings 85

Section 9: Figures and Diagrams 85

Section 10: Closing comments 85

STUDY AID 9: Paragraphs **87**

Section 1: Opening comments 89

Section 2: Paragraph Openings 89

Section 3: Structural features 90

Section 4: Stylistic features 91

Section 5: Paragraph Endings 91

Section 6: The advantages (and disadvantages) of brief sentences 92

Section 7: The advantages (and disadvantages) of long sentences 92

Section 9: Punctuation 92

Section 10: Closing comments 93

STUDY AID 10: **Conclusions** 95

Section 1: Opening comments 97

Section 2: Types of conclusion 97

Section 3: Characteristics of a good conclusion 98

Section 4: Improving conclusions 98

Section 5: Addenda 99

Section 6: Appendices 99

Section 7: Footnotes 100

Section 8: Bibliographies 100

Section 9: Overall structure of Bibliographies 101

Section 10: Closing comments 101

Appendix 1: Overview of an effective assignment/essay structure 102

STUDY AID 11: **Proof Reading** **105**

Section 1: Opening comments 107

Section 2: The stages of proof reading 108

Section 3: The advantages of proof reading aloud 109

Section 4: Things to look out for when proof reading 109

Section 5: Evaluating proof reading 110

Section 6: Clichés 110

Section 7: Closing comments 111

Appendix 1: The relationship between proof reading and essay drafting 112

STUDY AID 12: **Exam Skills** **113**

Section 1: Opening comments 115

Section 2: Qualities required 115

Section 3: Common reasons for failure in exam preparation 116

Section 4: More reasons for exam failure 117

Section 5: Exam preparation 118

Section 6: Approaching exam questions 119

Section 7: Time management 119

Section 8: Answering exam questions 120

Section 9: Structuring exam answers 121

Section 10: Closing comments 121

Appendix 1: A list of *'instruction words'* used in exams 122

Appendix 2: *'A'* Level Grades 122

Appendix 3: *'Question Dissection'* 123

Appendix 4: Planning to answer exam questions 123

Appendix 5: Handling Documentary Evidence 124

PART 2: REVISION AIDS **125**

REVISION AIDS 1: Foundation Level **127**

1) DAEJ 129

2) DEARS 130

3) DEEPS 131

4) GCSE Business Studies Project Checklist 132

5) How best to analyse poetry? 133

6) How best to criticise poetry? 135

7) How best to handle historical sources? 137

8) How best to interpret statistics? 138

9) What is History? 139

10) What makes a great life? 141

REVISION AIDS 2: Intermediate Level **143**

1) CESSPITTS Analysis 145

2) Contents of a Business Plan 146

3) How best to handle Business Case Studies? 148

4) How to learn formulae without panicking? 150

5) Key phrases for Sociology essays 153

6) Sociological Perspectives 155

7) The difference between a *'sound'* and an *'unsound'* theory 158

8) The stages of questionnaire design 159

9) The *'Syllabus Summary Method'* (SSM) 161

REVISION AIDS 3: Higher Level **163**

1) Ethics in Business 167

2) Financial Statements 166

3) How best to interpret sources? 171

4) The contrast between Modernism and Post-Modernism 176

5) The *'Dialectical Method'* of argumentation 178

6) The *'Fifteen Methods'* of verification 179

7) The *'Longsight Pathway'* 182

8) The role of Human Resources in Workforce Planning 187

ADDITIONAL NOTE: THE LEVELS OF PLAGIARISM **188**

BIBLIOGRAPHY **191**

INTRODUCTION

When embarking upon a career as a Private Tutor (**October 1990**) I repeatedly found that many of my students were lacking in basic study skills. Precious time, which would have been far better spent imparting subject knowledge, had instead to be given over to the provision of these skills. The following two decades saw the continuation of this same problem and has now led to the production of this new and thoroughly revised edition (the first having been produced in 1994.)

Advantage Study Skills seeks to improve the performance of teachers and students (operating at the Sixth Form, College or University level) as well as those returning to learning after a long gap. A variety of topics is covered, along with helpful Tables, Summaries and Illustrative Guides.

Advantage Study Skills spurs the genuine student on to exam success and provides a step-by-step guide to tackling any assignment. It's an invaluable resource, proving its worth repeatedly.

Richard Smith (Private Tutor) May 2013

PART 1: STUDY AIDS

STUDY AID 1: NOTE-TAKING SKILLS

Contents

AIMS

SECTION 1: Opening comments

SECTION 2: Reasons for note-taking

SECTION 3: The characteristics of good and bad notes

SECTION 4: Nucleated notes

SECTION 5: The advantages and disadvantages of nucleated notes

SECTION 6: Sequential notes

SECTION 7: The advantages and disadvantages of sequential notes

SECTION 8: Abbreviations

SECTION 9: Closing comments

APPENDICES

APPENDIX 1: Sample *'Contents Page'*

APPENDIX 2: The development of nucleated notes

APPENDIX 3: Fifty-two standards abbreviations

Aims

The study skills learnt in this section should enable the student to: -

- Understand the purpose of note-taking

- Begin writing good quality notes

- Avoid repeating any source material *'ad verbatim'* (word for word)

- Distinguish between nucleated and sequential notes

- Know the advantages and disadvantages of nucleated and sequential notes

- Distinguish between good and bad note-taking

- Develop an effective storage system

Section 1: Opening Comments

NOTES are the written summaries of lectures, literature and any other form of audio-visual material.

NOTE-TAKING: the activity of compiling notes (often in an orderly manner) to store information and to aid revision

Section 2: Reasons for Note-Taking

Note-Taking serves to: -

2.1   Draw together different ideas

2.2   Make sense of a written text

2.3   Organise information into a logical sequence

2.4   Provide the basis for a more complete written work

2.5   Record key facts

2.6   Provide a succinct summary of what's been said or written

2.7   Show the connections between certain points

2.8   Record original ideas and thoughts

2.9   Help formulate conclusions

2.10 Keep the mind alert and active

2.11 Trigger or jog the memory

2.12 Clarify thinking

2.13 Focus attention

2.14 Assist reference and revision

2.15 Aid the assimilation and learning of new information

Note-taking should only rarely be used to take things down `ad verbatim` (word for word)

Section 3: The Characteristics of Good and Bad Notes

	Good Notes are:	Bad Notes are:
3.1	Dated and numbered	Undated
3.2	Brief, concise and easy to read	Complicated and difficult to read
3.3	Clearly structured into relevant '*headed*' sections	Lacking in structure, with little or no headed sections
3.4	Clearly presented	Poorly presented
3.5	Separated into pertinent paragraphs	Lacking in paragraphs
3.6	Neatly written (or word-processed)	Badly written/word processed
3.7	Easily understood	Poorly understood
3.8	Made on appropriate stationery	Made on poor quality stationery
3.9	Readily accessible	Difficult to find
3.10	Relevant	Irrelevant
3.11	Clear in showing any relationship between ideas	Muddled in showing any relationship between ideas
3.12	Accurate in the use of diagrams and tables	Inaccurate in the use of diagrams and tables
3.13	Well-spaced	Poorly spaced
3.14	Selective when using quotes	Selects irrelevant quotes
3.15	Able to separate main ideas	Unable to separate main ideas
3.16	Able to record key definitions	Unable to record key definitions
3.17	Able to assist recall	Unable to assist recall
3.18	Able to skilfully highlight key points	Unable to highlight key points
3.19	Able to summarise complex information in a highly memorable form	Unable to summarise complex information, preferring repeat things '*ad verbatim*'
3.20	Safely filed away	Not safely filed away

N.B Should many notes be made then a *'Contents Page'* is best placed at the beginning **(Appendix 1, p.23).**

All pages should be numbered for easier reference.

Section 4: Nucleated Notes

Nucleated notes begin from a central reference point then move outward in linear branches, **(Appendix 2, p.24).** Often referred to as *'Spider Diagrams,'* stages in their development consist of: -

4.1   **The central reference point,** *e.g.* the essay title, or a word summing up the main topic.

4.2   **Main-Branching** – main ideas are recorded as if they were branches from the central reference point.

4.3   **Sub-Branching** – any related ideas are recorded.

4.4   **Concluding** – any further causal connections are noted down before a conclusion is made

Section 5: The Advantages and Disadvantages of Nucleated Notes

	Advantages, they: -	Disadvantages, they: -
5.1	Act as a basis for sequential notes	Are unable to record large pieces of information
5.2	Assist creative thinking	Record information in a haphazard fashion
5.3	Are easily added to	Are often messy and therefore unintelligible
5.4	Record new ideas	May include irrelevant ideas
5.5	Tend to be brief	Can become far too long and meandering
5.6	Show causal relationships	May include irrelevant relationships

Section 6: Sequential Notes

Sequential notes record information in an ordered and logical sequence. To be good they need to: -

6.1   Display a coherent numbering order (or use bullet points)

6.2   Adopt the characteristics of good notes **(3.1-3.20)**

6.3   Be interspersed with Diagrams and Tables

6.4   Be well-spaced for easy insertion of any new material

6.5   Be written on A4 paper, placed in a loose-leafed folder (for easier addition of more material)

6.6   Have key points **highlighted** or underlined

6.7   Pick out the essential points from the source material

6.8 Use an asterisk * (placed within the margin) to draw the reader's attention to key points

6.9 Record sources of information as they're being used

6.10 Reinforce any previous information (with the addition of fresh ideas or newly discovered sources)

6.11 Separate different portions of information

6.12 Not be viewed as a *'work of art'*

6.13 Clearly define any creative ideas

6.14 Accurately record relevant quotes and citations

6.15 Good sequential notes should never contain: -

6.15.1 Unnecessary doodling

6.15.2 Irrelevant material

6.15.3 Lengthy illustrations

6.15.4 Long quotes

6.15.5 Repetitive information

Small *'bite-sized'* reminders (of the key points) can be used to further aid assimilation. They need always to be accessible to act as *'memory joggers.'* They are best noted down on envelope-sized cards or placed on relevant I.T facilities.

Section 7:
The Advantages and Disadvantages of Sequential Notes

	Advantages, they: -	Disadvantages, they: -
7.1	Facilitate cross-referencing	Can become easily cluttered
7.2	Are clearly ordered	May become far too big
7.3	Have a definite structure	May slow thinking
7.4	Record Diagrams, Tables and Charts	
7.5	Record detailed information	
7.6	Readily display chronological events	

Section 8: Abbreviations

Abbreviations form an essential part of note-taking. They consist of letters or symbols which represent longer words or symbols *e.g. 'Abbn'* for *'Abbreviation.'* Their main purpose is to facilitate note-taking and information storage. **Abbns** must be: -

8.1   **Consistent** – each **abbn** should have only ONE meaning, otherwise confusion will result. However, some exceptions do exist, *e.g.*

         C   =   Copyright
         C   =   about a certain date
         C19   =   Nineteenth Century

         As far as **Abbns** are concerned the context (the surrounding information) is of the utmost importance ensuring that the correct **abbn** is used. Only one **abbn** should be consistently used to represent a term in the same set of notes, *e.g. 'not known'* should be represented only by **N/K** (not known) and not also by **D/K** (don't know) or **U/K** (unknown). To do otherwise would risk confusion and make a set of notes difficult to follow.

8.2   **Limited** – except for very technical or scientific subjects, **abbns** should never be used in essays or any other piece of literature. They're meant only for note-taking.

8.3   **Standardised** – where possible, standard (officially recognised) **abbns** (symbols) should always be used in preference to those which are personally fashioned.

8.4   **Uniform** – One type of **Abbn** and symbol must be used throughout, e.g. *'C'* should have only one – not two or three different meanings within a given set of notes, *and e.g. 'circa' (around) not century* which should be denoted by a different symbol e.g. *'Cent.'* Hence, one should avoid **abbns** like *'C21C'* meaning *'around the twenty-first century.'* Instead, it should read *'C21Cent.'*

Abbns can save time and improve the quality of note-taking – especially during lectures.

The speed of change within the English language tends only to worsen matters *i.e.* **'App'** can mean **Appendix,** or a technological **Application** on some electronic device.

Because the English Language is constantly evolving new **abbns** will invariably come into vogue. Their worth always lies in their usefulness; should an **abbn** ever lose its clear meaning then its best left to quietly fall out of usage.

Section 9: Closing Comments

Without good notes exam success is well-nigh impossible. They're the *'workaday tools'* for every student and should be adopted at the beginning of the academic year. Should they be unheeded and left in a dishevelled heap then the student will find exam revision far more difficult. Finally, it's worth remembering, that: -

GOOD NOTES = EASIER EXAM REVISION + BETTER EXAM GRADES

Appendix 1: Sample 'Contents Page'

....

....

....

....

....

....

....

....

....

....

....

....

....

....

....

....

....

....

....

....

....

....

....

....

....

Appendix 2: The Development of Nucleated Notes

Nucleated notes may be recorded in the form of a *'Spider Diagram'*

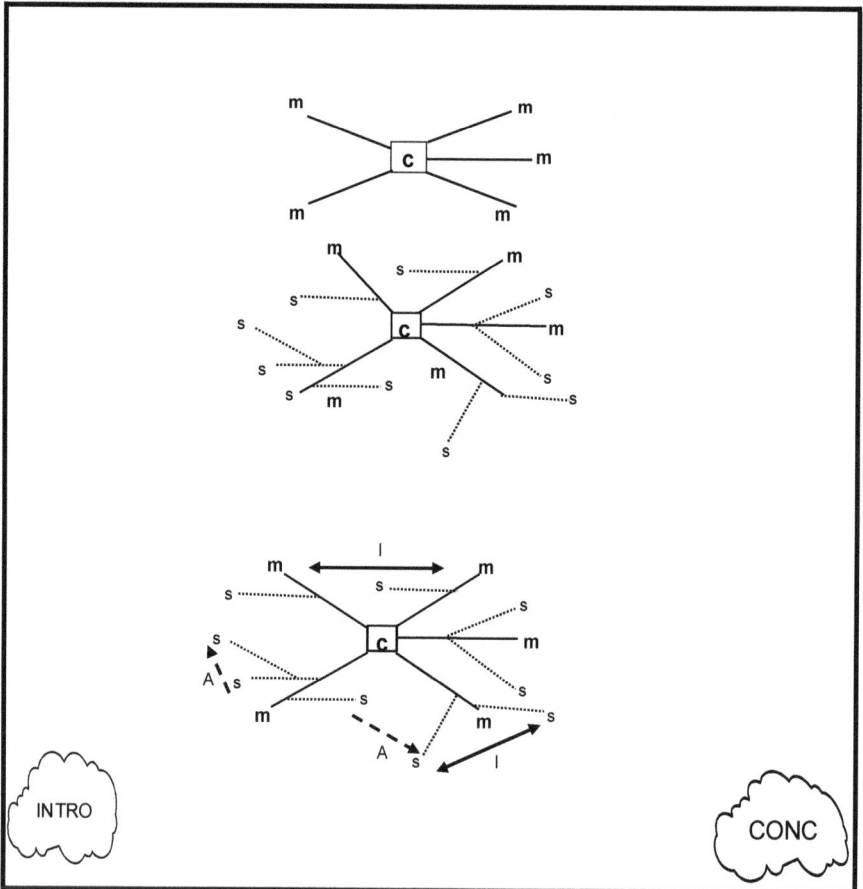

KEY

INTRO = Introduction or (introductory comments)
C = Central Reference Point *e.g.* Hitler's rise to power
M = Main Branches *e.g.* main causes of Hitler's rise to power
S = Sub-Branches *e.g.* secondary causes of Hitler's rise to power
A = Cause and effect relationships *e.g.* the great depression & German voting behaviour
I = Circular feedback relationships *e.g.* Nazi propaganda fuelling Hitler's rise to power
CONC = Conclusion (or Closing Comments)

Appendix 3: Fifty-Two Standard Abbreviations

	Meanings		Meanings
A, Ans	Answer, in answer to	**Intro**	Introduction, introduce
A-Z	From beginning to end	**Loccit**	In the place already cited or stated
Abbn	Abbreviation	**Mat.**	Material
A/P	As previously	**MS(S)**	Manuscript(s)
App(s)	Appendix, appendices, technological application(s)	**N/A**	Not applicable
ASAP	As soon as possible	**NB**	Note well, is of importance
C, c	Copyright	**ND**	No date of publication
Cent	Century	**NP**	New paragraph
c. circa	Around a certain date *e.g.* c1991	**OP cit**	In a work already cited
c.f.	Compare, in this context	**P. PP.**	Page, Pages
Ch(s)	Chapter(s)	**Para(s)**	Paragraph, paragraphs
Col(s)	Column(s)	**Passim**	Throughout the work
Conc(s)	Conclusion(s), concentration(s) *e.g.* of a liquid	**PS**	Post script – added after the main body of writing
Def	Define, definition	**PTO**	Please turn over
Ed.	Editor	**Q, QP,**	Question or quotation on page
Edn	Edition	**Q.V.**	Which see (used in cross reference)
e.g.	For example,	**Ref**	Reference, with reference to
et al	And others, *e.g.* Jones et al	**Rev**	Revised by, revision, Reverend
etc.	And so, on, continuing	**(sic)**	This is so, to guarantee
et seq.	And following *e.g.* p 64 et seq.	**Stet**	As it sounds, do not alter
f	To the finish *e.g.* Luke 9:3f.	**Tra/s**	Translator(s) translation(s)
fig	Figure, diagram	**V(s)**	Verse(s)
fl	Follow on	**Vol (s)**	Volume(s)
Fol(s)	Folio(s)	**W/A**	When appropriate
IBID	In the same work, as previously indicated	**W/O**	Without, *e.g.* W/O cream
i.e.	That is, such as		

STUDY AID 2: REVISION SKILLS

Contents

AIMS

SECTION 1: Opening comments

SECTION 2: Types of research

SECTION 3: Memory techniques

SECTION 4: Reasons for failure

SECTION 5: The relationship between subject areas and different learning methods

SECTION 6: Closing comments

APPENDICES

APPENDIX 1: The Learning process

APPENDIX 2: Two possible rates of learning

APPENDIX 3: Example of a *'Revision Timetable'*

Aims

The study skills learnt in this section should enable the student to: -

- Focus upon a variety of immediate and long-term goals

- Prioritise their work

- Apply particularly helpful study techniques

- Distinguish between *'primary'* and *'secondary'* research

- Distinguish between *'qualitative'* and *'quantitative'* data

- Understand that the learning process follows a series of four stages

- Avoid any last-minute *'cramming'*

Section 1: Opening Comments

Interest in the subject and a desire to pass should motivate study.

1.   To increase these qualities it's important to devise: -

1:1   Long term goals *e.g.* to aid career prospects

1:2   Short term goals *e.g.* to fulfil assignment deadlines

1:3   Immediate goals *e.g.* to locate relevant literature for the assignment

2.   The above goals must follow the Mnemonic *'RAMP,'* meaning they must be:

2:1   **R**ealistic

2:2   **A**ttainable

2:3   **M**easurable (not always possible with long-term goals)

2:4   **P**rioritised between: -

2:4:1   What **MUST** be done**?**

2:4:2   What **MAY** be done?

2:4:3   What **MUST NOT** be done?

Section 2: Types of Research

Primary Research (known also as *'Field Research'*) – where *'primary'* (new and fresh) data is gathered through appropriate research methods, *e.g.* a street survey of shoppers

Secondary Research (known also as *'Desk Research'*) – where *'secondary'* (previously gathered) data is assessed – this data has been taken from others who've completed their own primary research and subsequently made those results known. Interested parties then choose to access these results to add to their own data.

A further difference arises with *'Quantitative'* and *'Qualitative'* data. The former represents data expressed in numeric (or statistical) form *e.g.* Census Returns. The latter is expressed in non-numeric form *e.g.* transcripts of in-depth interviews.

Any major project will require most, if not all the above types of research and data gathering. Unless confidentiality is a statutory requirement (as in the case of child research) or security reasons demand otherwise, all sources of data must be fully acknowledged.

Section 3: Memory Techniques

3.1 Perhaps the best study technique is that defined followed mnemonic term *'MACRO.'*

M: MEMORY – aided by the **RAM** technique: -

R: Repetition of visual aids and tables

A: Association – often in the form of *'nonsense'* sayings *e.g. 'Normal Norms'*

M: Memory joggers, *e.g.* **R**ichard **of Y**ork **G**ave **B**attle **I**n **V**ain (representing the colours of the rainbow – red, orange, yellow, green, blue, indigo and violet)

A: AIMS – these are clearly subdivided into *'immediate term'* (*e.g.* passing tomorrow's test), *'short term'* (*e.g.* Passing next year's exam), *'medium term'* (*e.g.* gaining access to a good university) *'long term'* (*e.g.* gaining a good university degree), or *'very long term'* (*e.g.* gaining entrance into a lucrative professional career)

C: Concentration – asking relevant questions to gain greater focus on the relevant subject *e.g. 'who, what, where, when, why and how?'*

R: Review and Recall – asking friends, teachers, family members or fellow students to test one's knowledge of a topic

O: Organisation – devising a timetable which allows for both study and leisure periods

3.2 Three separate *'hour-long'* study periods punctuated by five minute breaks each hour in the morning is often the most effective way to become familiar with difficult topics. To add variety, different areas may be studied in each separate hour. Afternoon and evening should be confined to lighter reading, or for the *"brushing up"* of notes. Plenty of time must be left for sleep.

3.3 Learning is more effective when following these four stages: -

Stage 1, Familiarisation: Read through a few general texts to gain a broader view of the subject and the challenges it presents

Stage 2, Assimilation: Highlight specific topics and take relevant notes

Stage 3, Plateau: Rest, take a week or two's break from the subject, allowing it plenty of time to digest in the subconscious mind

Stage 4, Peak Knowledge: Fill in any remaining gaps in knowledge by: -
- Checking the facts
- Evaluating (assessing the significance of) the information gained
- Revising and summarising the information gained

By the time the *'peak period'* of learning is reached, the information should be soundly known and understood.

These stages are illustrated in **Appendix 1**

Section 4: Reasons for Failure

Failure to study effectively could be as the result of: -

4.1   Environmental factors, including: -

4.1.1   Strange surroundings and people

4.1.2   Home sickness

4.1.3   Poor living accommodation

4.1.4   Lack of guidance from teaching staff

4.1.5   Miscellaneous distractions *e.g.* noise caused by a nearby road drill

4.2   Personal factors, including: -

4.2.1   Accident, illness and bereavement

4.2.2   Spiritual problems (to do with religious faith)

4.2.3   Relationship problems

4.2.4   Financial problems

4.3   Poor study technique, including: -

4.3.1   A failure to devise and follow a structured timetable

4.3.2   Last minute *'cramming,'* (which creates unnecessary fatigue and feelings of panic)

4.3.3   Over-concentration upon some subjects at the expense of others

4.3.4   A failure to quickly deal with any problems

4.3.5   A denial that any learning problems exist

Appendix 2 (see **p.34**) shows that poor study techniques can lead to an uneven rate of learning.

Section 5: The Relationship between Subject Areas and Different Learning Methods

A subject area is often best grasped by a suitable learning method (or mixture of methods) as seen in this Table.

SUBJECT AREA	LEARNING METHOD
Accountancy or statistical formulae	*'Pretty Polly & practice'* – this means learning by *'hearing, repeating and doing.'*
Basic facts	Colourful fact cards with cross references to relevant information sources, (in either alphabetical or syllabus order). Diagrams and visual summaries may also be used.
Case Studies	Repeated reading, idea association, (where names are associated with an idea (*e.g.* Freud being associated with the idea of the subconscious) evaluating and summarizing on either a private or team basis.
Causal relationships	Memory equations $(x \rightarrow y)$
Creative work	*'Thought showers'* and *'learning by doing'*
Diagrams and Tables	*'Flow chart,'* summarizing each step and employing arrows ($\downarrow$) between each one.
Discussion topics	Comparative tables which list the positives and negatives.
Study skills	*'Pretty polly'* and practice. Using *'tally points'* to monitor the degree of progress, beginning with (**I**) which means *'very weak'* and progressing onto (**LHI**) which means *'very good.'*

Each subject area requires a different approach; one learning method will be suitable in one instance but not in another.

Section 6: Closing Comments

The above techniques will only work where a robust level of knowledge already exists. They cannot be a substitute for knowledge which isn't there. Such knowledge is best accumulated during the early stages of a course. A closely followed Revision Timetable is an absolute necessity (**Appendix 3, p.33**).

Appendix 1: The Learning Process

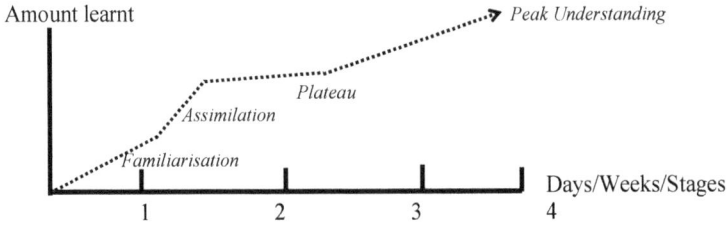

This graph shows the four stages which occur in a typical learning process. It highlights the diverse rate of learning which occurs at each stage.

Appendix 2: Two Possible Rates of Learning

Graph A

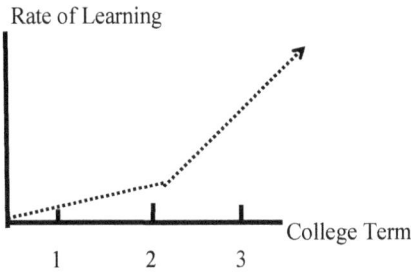

Graph B

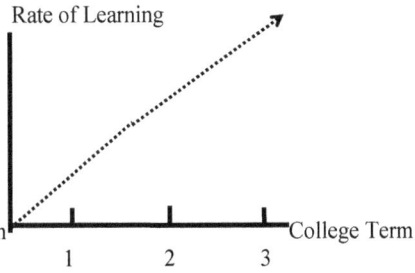

Graph A shows the rate of learning which occurs over an academic year when poor study techniques lead to last minute cramming. In contrast, **Graph B** shows the more balanced rate which takes place when good study techniques are followed.

Appendix 3: Example of a 'Revision Timetable'

The following example is geared to Advanced Level Students studying three subjects and having one rest day each work.

Step 1: Arrange the subjects being studied into alphabetical order, *e.g.* English, Politics and Sociology

Step 2: Assign code numbers to these subjects, *e.g.* History is assigned the number *'1,'* Politics the number *'2'* and Sociology is assigned the number *'3'*

Step 3: Assign *'various other activities'* the code number *'4.'* (These activities may include practising assignments, catching up with previous work or improving one's planning and study skills)

Step 4: Draw up the following timetable – where the numbers correspond to those mentioned above. Each number represents **45-90** minutes of revision activity (depending upon whether the revision takes place within Term Time or in a holiday period.)

Day/Week	Week 1	Week 2	Week 3	Week 4
Monday	1234	2341	3412	4123
Tuesday	2341	3412	4123	1234
Wednesday	3412	4123	1234	2341
Thursday	4123	1234	2412	3412
Friday	1234	2412	3412	4123
Saturday	Discretionary	Discretionary	Discretionary	Discretionary
Sunday	Rest	Rest	Rest	Rest

Step 5: Follow the H.E. (hard to easy) order in which the harder topics (shown by the underlined numbers) are covered at the start of the week when tiredness is less of a problem. Leave one day for discretionary or *'catch-up'* work.

The main advantage of such a *'Revision Timetable'* is that it contains the right mixture of structure and flexibility, leaving space for personal discretion. It does <u>not</u> suggest that all revision must be done within a period of four weeks. This type of *'Timetable'* can be adopted at any time – even months before final exams take place.

STUDY AID 3: THINKING SKILLS

Contents

AIMS

SECTION 1: Opening comments

SECTION 2: The characteristics of effective thinking

SECTION 3: Obstacles to effective thinking

SECTION 4: Symptoms of poor thinking

SECTION 5: Ways to improve thinking

SECTION 6: Handling evidence

SECTION 7: The three parts of an argument

SECTION 8: Developing an argument

SECTION 9: Modifying an argument

SECTION 10: Strengthening an argument

SECTION 11: Closing comments

Aims

The study skills learnt in this section should enable the student to: -

- Understand and memorise the characteristics of effective thinking

- Remove obstacles to effective thinking

- Avoid the common flaws in poor thinking

- Improve thinking ability

- Handle evidence competently

- Develop, modify and strengthen an argument

- Realise that quality in thinking can determine quality of personal character

Section 1: Opening Comments

Effective thinking (or effective reasoning) is the ability to logically *'think through'* and conclude based upon a proper understanding of all the available evidence. Effective reasoning tends to improve the quality of any work and creates other numerous (often personally) beneficial results, including assistance with decision-making.

Section 2: The Characteristics of Effective Thinking

Effective thinking involves: -

2.1 Accepting the challenge that an innovation may generate fresh ideas.

2.2 Arriving at original solutions to pressing problems

2.3 Asking questions and formulating logical answers

2.4 Comprehending, interpreting and wisely applying any relevant data

2.5 Defining words clearly

2.6 Drawing out the full implications of any concept or argument

2.7 Expressing instinctive feelings using images, symbols and words

2.8 Expressing well-founded and carefully chosen opinions

2.9 Avoiding both complacency and excessive worry

2.10 Impartially considering all sides of an argument

2.11 Maintaining good communication with all relevant parties

2.12 Making firm decisions based upon the available facts

2.13 Remaining open-minded whilst testing everyday assumptions

2.14 Stepping back from blindly following public opinion

2.15 Suggesting causal relationships

Effective thinking involves some degree of originality, an ability to focus upon the detail and some skill in interpersonal relationships. However, it's possible to think of exceptions, *i.e.* Mozart's genius in music was equally matched by his genius for making enemies! His social skills were reputedly very limited.

Section 3: Obstacles to Effective Thinking

Obstacles to effective thinking may include: -

3.1   A dislike of challenge

3.2   Lack of confidence

3.3   Fondness for holding on to comforting illusions *e.g.* hard work isn't necessary

3.4   An unwillingness to accept (or handle) responsibility

3.5   Quirks of character *e.g.* a person may be *'a natural scatter-brain'*

3.6   Poor education

3.7   Time constraints, making one *'too busy to think'*

3.8   Personal stress *i.e.* concerning work and family pressures

3.9   Physical and mental ill health

3.10   Emotional distress due to a traumatic event *e.g.* bereavement

Section 4: Symptoms of Poor Thinking

Common symptoms of poor thinking include: -

4.1   A misleading use of similes *e.g.* *"whiter than white"*

4.2   Making conclusions not based upon the evidence *e.g.* *"Toads are mostly green, they therefore eat green peas"*

4.3   Making dogmatic assertions *e.g.* *"All doctors have bad handwriting"*

4.4   Resorting to supposedly infallible authorities to impress others, yet failing to verify them *e.g.* *"the priest says"* or *"professor so and so states"*

4.5   The adoption of *"the causal fallacy"* where it's assumed that if **'A'** and **'B'** occur together then **'A → B.'** However, the two could have been inter-related through another cause *e.g.* **'C → A + B,'** or **'B → A'.** An example of this is the myth that soap bubbles produce cleaner clothes.

4.6   The casual acceptance of groundless assumptions *e.g.* *"All history is the history of the class struggle."*

4.7   The forming of a generalisation from one (but often unrepresentative) example. Convenient cases may be selected to justify already established prejudices *e.g.* *"All short people are bossy because I knew a colleague who was only five feet tall and she was certainly bossy!"*

4.8   Failing to form adequate, verifiable conclusions from the original argument, *e.g. "All school children are lazy, but Peter works hard."*

4.9   Lazily ignoring obvious inconsistencies – failing to *'think a thing through'* adequately *e.g.* the lawyer's trick question, *"Have you stopped beating your wife yet?"*

4.10   The implementation of a tautological argument (a needless repetition). Here, the same thing is said twice to make it more credible *e.g. "Ben has fair hair because he is blond" or "this <u>corpse</u> is <u>dead!</u>"* Such contradictions may not be easy to spot as they can often be widely separated in a piece of writing.

4.11   A total (or near total) lack of verification *e.g. "I know life exists on Pluto"*

4.12   The use of insult or innuendo in place of argument, *e.g. "That useless so and so said ..."*

Section 5: Ways to Improve Thinking

To improve thinking it's necessary to: -

5.1   Avoid any of the above flaws **(4.1 - 4.12)**

5.2   Establish a direct connection between basic assumptions, lines of reasoning and conclusions

5.3   Find the interrelationship between various factors

5.4   Keep an open mind for if possible

5.5   Seek out all relevant information

5.6   Take time before rushing to conclusions

The following techniques, when used, can improve effective thinking: -

5.7.1 **THOUGHT SHOWERS** – using *'free writing'* or *'nucleated notes,'* where ideas are written down in random order as they come to mind. These ideas are <u>not</u> edited as their intention is to encourage *'divergent creative'* rather than *'convergent lateral'* thinking.

5.7.2 **COLTS** – a mnemonic, useful when deciding which subject or topic to choose: -

<u>C</u>irculating (rearranging) important material on cards

<u>O</u>pen-minded outlook concerning subject or topic

<u>L</u>ooking more closely at a specific subject or topic

<u>T</u>alking matters over with colleagues and tutors

<u>S</u>ifting through and summarising relevant information

5.7.3 **TRIAD** – a mnemonic, useful in developing all aspects of the student's personality:

Temperament – building upon helpful personal habits and dealing with unhelpful ones

Responsibility – accepting the consequences should things go wrong

Integrity – being completely trustworthy and giving full attention to detail

Ability – personal capacity or inner aptitude which may improve with practice

Delegation – able to hand over responsibility to others

5.8 Using *'Improve Your Memory'* techniques. Some may well be helpful, whilst others may prove dubious and expensive. Great care should be taken before following up any media advertising which promises a sudden and dramatic improvement in memory skills. There's also the added point that a technique which may work for one person may prove useless for another. People really do have different styles of learning.

5.9 Thinking is also improved by adopting a suitable learning style. Whilst some learn by *'seeing,'* (visual learning, which is important in art and design), others learn by *'hearing,'* (auditory learning which is important in art music) or by *'doing'* (Kinaesthetic learning which is important in a skill like dry stonewalling). Different subjects therefore require different learning styles, (see also **p.32**).

Section 6: Handling Evidence

To competently handle evidence, it's best to: -

6.1 Gain as much understanding as possible of the known facts and theories

6.2 Consider the evidence from all possible angles

6.3 Consider alternative valid evidence

6.4 Look at examples and ask *"Are they typical?"*

6.5 Look for the *'underlying'* as well as the *'obvious'* meanings

6.6 Rely upon many sources rather than just one text

6.7 Take an argument to its logical ending, seeing whether any flaws are revealed along the way

6.8 Combine imagination with intuition and intelligent deduction

6.9 Avoid *'cloudy'* expressions and unclear terminology, *e.g. 'on-going situation'*

6.10 Avoid emotional words and phrases *e.g. "terrific"*

6.11 Avoid *'soft'* euphemisms *e.g. "creative accounting"*

6.12   Avoid statements which cannot be verified with sound facts e.g. *"The moon is made of green cheese"*

Section 7: The Three Parts of an Argument

There are two types of logical argument, each one of which can be divided into three parts: -

AN INDUCTIVE ARGUMENT

This line of reasoning begins with fresh (raw) primary or secondary data *e.g.* official census results and begins to draw conclusions from it.

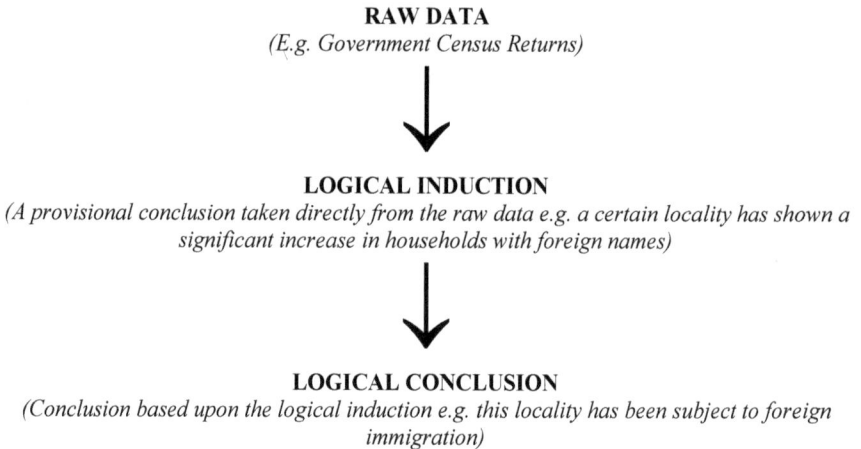

RAW DATA
(E.g. Government Census Returns)

↓

LOGICAL INDUCTION
(A provisional conclusion taken directly from the raw data e.g. a certain locality has shown a significant increase in households with foreign names)

↓

LOGICAL CONCLUSION
(Conclusion based upon the logical induction e.g. this locality has been subject to foreign immigration)

A DEDUCTIVE ARGUMENT

A deductive approach is a line of reasoning which begins with a specific assumption, argument, premise or theoretical principle and begins to draw conclusions from it.

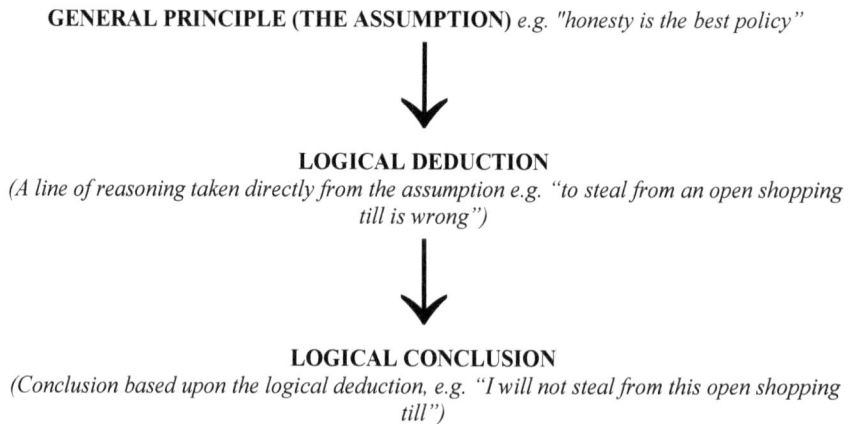

GENERAL PRINCIPLE (THE ASSUMPTION) *e.g. "honesty is the best policy"*

↓

LOGICAL DEDUCTION
(A line of reasoning taken directly from the assumption e.g. "to steal from an open shopping till is wrong")

↓

LOGICAL CONCLUSION
(Conclusion based upon the logical deduction, e.g. "I will not steal from this open shopping till")

In practice, both types of argument can be used in one project. Fresh (or raw) data may challenge certain assumptions, whilst assumptions can often lead to the interpretation of fresh data. Students in Higher Education are expected to apply both approaches, whenever necessary. Usually, they will begin with an *'inductive argument'* whose *'logical conclusion'* will become the *'general principle'* of a *'deductive argument.'*

Section 8: Developing an Argument

A logical argument is one which is presented in a readily understood and persuasive way. It can be developed even further when it: -

8.1   Derives from an assumption, *e.g. "Hunger causes laziness"* and *"All hungry school children are lazy."*

8.2   Fits in with other arguments *e.g. "Some school children from particular social backgrounds are often lazy. This is because such backgrounds are often chaotic, resulting in those children arriving at school having had no breakfast."*

8.3   Leads naturally to a logical conclusion *e.g. "Lazy school children need to be checked by the teacher that they've had breakfast before their arrival at school."*

Section 9: Modifying an Argument

Modifying an argument can be done by: -

9.1   **CONDITIONING** the application, *e.g. "All school children are lazy in subjects they dislike."*

9.2   **LIMITING** the application *e.g. "All school children are lazy on Friday afternoons."*

9.3   **QUALIFYING** the application, *e.g. "All school children are lazy when they dislike their teacher."*

9.4   **WEAKENING** the application, *e.g. "All school children tend to be lazy."*

Such modifications prevent the student from being too dogmatic or too generalised in his/her assertions.

Section 10: Strengthening an Argument

An argument is strengthened by giving valid reasons for its views. This is best achieved by: -

10.1   Taking ideas from recognised authorities; which must always be cited

10.2   Employing logical deductions – from the argument's premise to its conclusion

10.3   Offering primary (one's own) or secondary (other people's) factual evidence, when required

10.4   Using vivid illustrations to generate mental pictures, enabling a better *'grasp'* of the points being made

Section 11: Closing Comments

11.3   Be wary of any psychological or relaxation techniques which encourage the *'Turning off the mind.'* Not using the mind could well lead to some form of manipulation by outside parties. There is also the common sense point that minds are there to be used. Failure to employ them can hinder learning. *'Switching of the mind'* doesn't always produce the form of relaxation that helps one to think better.

11.2   Effective thinking forms the basis of all academic and personal competence and leads to effective action.

11.3   Who we are as people is often communicated by our personality, which in turn is governed by our thinking.

STUDY AID 4: WRITING SKILLS

Contents

AIMS

SECTION 1: Opening comments

SECTION 2: The characteristics of effective writing

SECTION 3: The differences between the written and spoken word

SECTION 4: The *'Golden Rules'* to effective writing

SECTION 5: Preparing to write effectively

SECTION 6: Gaining precision when writing

SECTION 7: Things to avoid when writing

SECTION 8: The *'active'* and the *'passive'* voice

SECTION 9: Circumlocutions

SECTION 10: *'Signposting'*

SECTION 11: *'Signpost'* Words

SECTION 12: *'Link'* Words

SECTION 13: Closing comments

APPENDICES

APPENDIX 1: A *'communication chain'* and its vulnerability to *'noise'*

APPENDIX 2: The impressions formed by good and bad writing

Aims

The study skills learnt in this section should enable the student to: -

- Become familiar with a variety of writing styles

- Pick out the characteristics of effective writing

- Understand the contrasts between the written and spoken word

- Follow the *'golden rules'* of effective writing

- Employ *'link words'* and *'signposts'*

- Avoid those traits that make for bad writing

- Improve upon an initially poor writing style

Section 1: Opening Comments

Semantic skills are those which help gain artistry in words, shown in greater powers of expression and often leading to written work of a high standard.

The main types of writing are: -

1.1   Expository: to describe, explain, objectively argue with and comment upon a person or thing.

1.2   Expressive: to convey a sense of emotion – sometimes in poetical form.

1.3   Legal: used (often in detail) for constitutional rules, government regulations, organisational codes of practice and conditions of contract.

1.4   Narrative: to recount an event or to tell a story.

1.5   Polemical Writing: to vigorously propagate (or demolish) a viewpoint; to expose an abuse or to provoke controversial discussion, is often characterised by the use of strong language.

All the above types of writing involve the transference of thoughts from the writer to the reader's mind, via the written word. Hence, as **Appendix 1** shows, a *'communication chain'* exists between the writer and his/her audience. At every point this *'chain'* may be broken by *'noise'* (which denotes any factor in either the writer or the reader which may hinder effective communication). *'Noise'* affecting the writer may include a poor choice of words, ill health or interruptions; whilst *'noise'* on the reader's part also includes a limited comprehension. The writer's role is to greatly reduce the amount of *'noise'* by acquiring and practising all the skills needed for effective writing. These are listed in **Section 2.**

Section 2: The Characteristics of Effective Writing

Effective writing is: -

2.1   Accurate

2.2   Adequate and concise

2.3   Appropriate

2.4   Balanced

2.5   Clearly expressed

2.6   Completeness

2.7   Consistent

2.8   Focussed

2.9   Impartial

2.10   Interesting

2.11   Orderly

2.12   Original

2.13   Persuasive

2.14   Pertinent

2.15   Precise

2.16   Relevant

2.17   Simple

2.18   Sincerity

2.19   Structurally sound

2.20   Well-balanced in its willingness to present both sides of an argument

2.21   Well-presented – using illustrations and diagrams

2.22   Well-defined – with a clear *'beginning,' 'middle'* and *'end'*

N.B: Not all the above characteristics need be present in one piece of writing, *i.e.* originality is hardly required in an Inland Revenue Tax Report. However, it's worth remembering most writing can create either a good or a bad impression, **(Appendix 2).**

Section 3:
The Differences Between the Written and Spoken Word

Writing differs from speaking because it: -

3.1   Demands clearer levels of expression simply because it's standing alone – unsupported by body language or facial expression

3.2   Is often more formal

3.3   Is slower and less spontaneous (people speak quicker than they write)

3.4   Is used less often in daily life

3.5   Requires the writer to make all the decisions regarding subject and style

3.6   Often takes longer to obtain feedback or constructive criticism

Section 4: The 'Golden Rules' to Effective Writing

Effective writing is deemed successful when it generates a good impression. Certain *'Golden Rules'* exist, which, when used, should result in a truly effective piece of writing, *i.e.* using: -

4.1   A concrete rather than an abstract expression

4.2   A single word rather than a circumlocution

4.3   An *'active'* rather than a *'passive'* voice

4.4   A *'Saxon'* rather than a *'Romance'* word *e.g. 'What will be will be'* instead of *'Que sera sera'*

4.6   An external aid whenever necessary *e.g.* A Dictionary, English grammar book or Thesaurus. Also, electronic *'helps'* via the computer or mobile phone

4.7   A familiar rather than a far-fetched word

4.8   Critical feedback to further improve one's writing skill

4.9   A clear and concise meaning rather than an ambiguous one

4.10   Modern information technology whenever possible *i.e.* word processing in place of handwriting

Application of these *'Golden Rules'* is seen elsewhere in this study. Generally, it's wise to remember that <u>the greater the pleasure the author has in the writing, the greater the likelihood of it having a beneficial effect upon the reader.</u>

Section 5: Preparing to Write Effectively

Preparing to write effectively involves: -

5.1 Gathering relevant information

5.2 Knowing there's something worth saying in the first place

5.3 Remaining true to the focus and staying with it

5.4 Resisting the temptation to wander away from the focus

5.5 Deciding upon the most advantageous style and persevering with it

5.6 Consciously bearing in mind the audience for whom it's written

5.7 Avoiding unnecessary distraction

5.8 Taking care to say exactly what needs to be said, in as simple and succinct a manner as possible

5.9 Being realistic *i.e.* it may not be a perfect piece of work the first-time around

Section 6: Gaining Precision When Writing

To gain precision the writer should: -

6.1 Aim for a style which is **DLSV**, **Direct, Lucid, Simple** and **Vigorous.**

6.2 Alternate long with short sentences and long with short paragraphs

6.3 <u>Always</u> document information sources – to avoid plagiarism

6.4 Guide the reader by using *'signpost'* and *'linking'* words (See **Sections 10** and **12**)

6.5 Be alert to the <u>sound</u> of what is being written – if it <u>sounds</u> good it probably <u>is good</u>

6.6 Be cautious about employing fashionable words that could quickly become out-dated, *e.g. 'collateral damage', 'game plan', 'teach-in'*

6.7 Be consistent in the use of past or present tense *e.g. "I will go to town and got on a bus."* (It should read *"I will go to town and get on a bus."*

6.8 Employ words that confer a clearer meaning, *e.g. 'imply'* not *'infer,' 'close'* not *'approximate,'* and *'superior to'* <u>not</u> *'superior than'*

6.9 Ensure every sentence has a *'doing'* word (verb) *i.e. "he <u>ran</u> to the bus stop"* as well as a *'describing'* (adjective) word *i.e. "he ran to the <u>concrete</u> bus stop"*

6.10 Ensure every sentence contains no tautology (needlessly repetitive phrase) *i.e. 'the round circle', 'the dead corpse', 'the final incident at the end'*

6.11 Give due care and attention to correct punctuation.

6.12 Use inverted commas around a proverbial expression or quotation *i.e. "He ran 'as fast as greased lightning' to the finishing line"*

6.13 Use imaginative illustration or *'visual'* language whenever appropriate. *i.e. "The nuclear explosion shone with the light of a million suns"*

6.14 Relate the subject matter to everyday life if this is relevant

6.15 Write nothing, if there's nothing to say

Section 7: Things to Avoid When Writing

When writing it's advisable to <u>avoid</u>: -

7.1 Abbreviations in written essays, *i.e. 'circa'* for *'about'* or *'viz'* for *'namely'*.

7.2 Clichés, *i.e. 'a fair and reasonable offer'*

7.3 Dogmatic assertions not collaborated by available evidence, *e.g. "Women are always treated as second class citizens in every society"*

7.4 *'Dead'* or unnecessary words *e.g. 'bunkum and balderdash'* or *'completely, utterly and very untrue'*

7.5 Obscenities (swearing or sexually explicit words) or personal idiosyncrasies, *e.g.* placing the phrase *'you know'* in every other sentence

7.6 Ambiguous expressions – using words which may have changed their meaning over time, *e.g. 'broadcast zone'* used to mean *'spreading the grain'* but now means *'spreading ideas'*

7.7 Needless lengthening of a word *e.g. 'method'* to *'methodology'*

7.8 Needless provocation which may lead directly to an outright objection, *e.g. "All short people are bossy"*

7.9 Excessive and unnecessary word usage (often called *'filling out'* or *'padding'*) *i.e. 'It is very interesting to note,' 'From certain particular viewpoints'*

7.10 Pomposity (grandiosity) – which tends only to engender annoyance, amusement or confusion, *e.g. "We have here the most fabulous, the most moving, the most enervating, the most stimulating, the most delectable act of our present time"*

7.11 Slander or libel, *e.g. "Sir Nigel Bloodaxe, the newspaper proprietor, is an absolute crook who lies and cheats to get his own way"*

7.12 Using slang (colloquialism) outside of dialogue, *e.g.* The report stated that the Firms Marketing Department were *'a waste of space'*

7.13 Technical jargon without prior explanation to non-specialist readers, e.g. *'The Monistic paradigm hypothesises that ...."*

7.14 Unnecessary compound words, *e.g. "Dickens manages to convince"* should be *"Dickens convinces"* and *"Shaw is trying to put over the point that"* should be *"Shaw points out that"*

7.15 Use of evasive circumlocutions (long winded, insincere, obscure and often grammatically incorrect phrases) unless necessary, *e.g. "A most interesting example of Modern Art"* which really means *"This painting is dreadful!"*

Section 8: The 'Active' and 'Passive' Voice

8.1 The **passive voice** avoids the use of the first person, *i.e. 'I', 'we', 'they.'* When using the passive voice, the object of an action precedes the verb. This tends to result in communication being rather verbose and artificial, as shown in the example below: -

"Colleagues and staff were asked to ..."

8.2 The **active voice** gives a sense of vitality and *'bite'* to the written word. The *'first person'* is used. When using the active voice the actual subject of the verb becomes the *'doer'* of the action. This results in the communication being more personal and immediate, as shown in the example below:

"I asked my colleagues and staff to"

Both *'voices'* can be used in a past, present or future tense.

Section 9: Circumlocutions

Circumlocutions are *'obscure phrases'* that tend to hide the real meaning of words. However, they may prove useful in certain circumstances when they serve to: -

9.1 *'Buy time'* – *i.e.* enabling the speaker to gain valuable minutes whilst searching for an adequate answer, *e.g. "It seems to me at this moment in time that there's possibly some questions which need to be raised about the accounts that you were responsible for providing"*

9.2 Cause the reader to pause and reflect upon what's been said

9.3 Avoid unnecessary repetition (which will only bore the reader)

9.4 Prevent simpler words or phrases from being used too often (which can create the impression of the writer being poorly educated or unintelligent)

9.5 Aid the process of diplomacy, *e.g. "It seems to me that what may be being said here does not accord too well with the available facts of the matter."* This is a polite way of saying *"You're lying."*

Section 10: 'Signposting'

Like *'link words'* signpost words serve to: -

10.1   Assist in the presentation of lists

10.2   Highlight what the writer has been talking about

10.3   Repeat key points within a work

10.4   Point to a stage in an argument

10.5   Reveal any new direction within an argument

Section 11: 'Signpost' Words

'Signposting' serves to remind the reader where they are within a given piece of writing and uses helpful words or phrases including: -

11.1   To begin with...

11.2   Another point...

11.3   Having seen...

11.4   As was stated...

11.5   Before discussing **X** we must first question **Y**...

11.6   But apart from that there is...

11.7   Finally...

11.8   Furthermore...

11.9   Having considered the argument...

11.10   Having questioned that point...

11.11   In short...

11.12   One final factor to be considered...

11.13   One further line of enquiry is...

11.14   To continue this point...

11.15   To sum up...

11.16   Whilst drawing matters to a close...

However, unlike *'link words,'* simple *'signpost words'* don't always join sentences together and can occur <u>within</u> as well as at the <u>beginning</u> of a sentence. They have only <u>one</u> main function which is to show a reader where they are in an argument or piece of writing.

Section 12: 'Link' Words

Link words are signpost words that assist sentence flow and are used to expand, qualify or contradict an argument, *i.e.*

12.1   Another point is...

12.2   At one level it's possible to see...

12.3   At the same time...

12.4   First we must dispense with...

12.5   There are perhaps other factors...

12.6   Certainly...

12.7   Conversely...

12.8   Hopefully...

12.9   In fact...

12.10 To understand...

12.11 Nevertheless...

12.12 None of this is to deny...

12.13 Not only that...

12.14 Of course...

12.15 On the other hand...

12.16 There are several problems with...

12.17 To aid comprehension, it's necessary to see that...

'Link words' act as a *'bridge'* from one sentence to the next and they help to keep the current thought/argument in the writer's mind. Unlike simple signpost words, they can only occur at the beginning of a sentence. The distinction between simple *'signpost'* and *'link'* words is a highly technical one and is perhaps only of interest to students doing a high level English course.

Shorter link words like *'certainly'* tend to convey more certainty than longer ones *e.g.* *'Certainly, this theory is valid'* In contrast, longer link words may convey a degree of hesitancy *e.g.* *'It's just about possible that this theory could be valid ...'*

'Link words' show the reader how to approach the next sentence, whilst they still *'link it in'* with the previous one, *e.g.* *"The unexpected findings posed a challenge to scientists. Hopefully, they would only require slight modifications to existing theory. On the other hand, they could require its complete replacement. None of this is to deny the possibility that they were the result of some technical error. Of course, there's always room for further debate."*

Section 13: Closing Comments

Constant practise will lead to a significant improvement in effective writing. Those with dyslexia (or similar conditions causing poor written presentation) may need to employ helpful resources *e.g.* specialised I.T facilities, different coloured reading paper or tinted spectacles. It is essential that such problems are diagnosed at an early stage, well before the need to sit an exam. The student should seek advice from the teacher, course manager, a specialist in *'inclusive learning'* or even from their student union representative.

Appendix 1:
A 'Communication Chain' and Its Vulnerability to 'Noise'

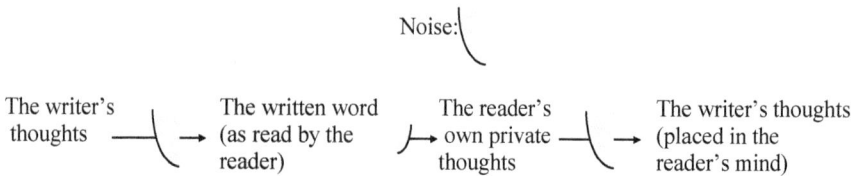

Noise:

| The writer's thoughts | → | The written word (as read by the reader) | → | The reader's own private thoughts | → | The writer's thoughts (placed in the reader's mind) |

It is important to note how *'noise'* can disrupt communication at every point. Good communication skills (like an ability to sum up key points) are one way of overcoming this problem.

Appendix 2:
The Impressions Formed by Good and Bad Writing

1. The main characteristics of a good writing style   **Impression created**

1.1	Clarity	Considerate
1.2	Correct spelling and punctuation	Well-educated
1.3	Good *"flow"* of words	→ Articulate
1.4	Correct use of grammar	Competent
1.5	Well-ordered	Organised
1.6	Convincing and well-presented arguments	Purposeful

2. The main characteristics of a bad writing style   **Impression created**

2.1	Illegible	Inconsiderate
2.2	Incorrect spelling and punctuation	Poorly-educated
2.3	Poor deployment of words	Incompetent
2.4	Incorrect use of grammar	Careless
2.5	Poorly ordered	Disorganised
2.6	Unconvincing or poorly presented arguments	Aimless

STUDY AID 5: FREE-WRITING

Contents

AIMS

SECTION 1: Opening comments

SECTION 2: Methodology

SECTION 3: Assessment of free-writing

SECTION 4: Advantages of free-writing

SECTION 5: Ways to improve writing style

SECTION 6: Closing comments

APPENDICES

APPENDIX 1: The stages of producing a written work

Aims

The study skills learnt in this section should enable the student to: -

- *"Free-write"* in a variety of styles

- Know the advantages of *'free-writing'*

- Generate thoughts and ideas relevant to the Assignment

- Remove any psychological inhibitions to writing

Section 1: Opening Comments

'Free-writing' is writing without editing. It's writing what we want, in the way we want and at the time we want, with no pauses to check what's been written. It's done with the express intention of enabling the writer to: -

1.1   Release their inner creativity

1.2   Find their *'inner voice'* or natural writing style

1.3   Generate new ideas

Section 2: Methodology

To *'free-write'* it's necessary to: -

2.1   Begin writing on anything of personal interest

2.2   Continue writing for 10-20 minutes without pause – either rapidly or slowly

2.3   <u>Carry on and not give up.</u> This is best achieved by repeating the last word (either in one's mind or on the paper) until a new word comes

2.4   Avoid worrying about the quality of the material being produced

2.5   Remain with only one topic within the allotted time or touch upon a whole range of topics as the mood allows

2.6   Correct the material the following day – having a fresh mind is always beneficial when a piece of work needs correcting

Section 3: Assessment of Free-writing

A general assessment of what's been written is best achieved with a fresh mind and involves:

3.1   Analyse the general structure

3.2   Underline <u>key words</u> or exceptionally <u>clear phrases</u>

3.3   Delete unwanted material

3.4   Highlight good points with a tick

3.5   Noting confused, unclear points with a question mark (?)

Section 4: The Advantages of Free-writing

'Free-writing' helps in: -

4.1   Bringing to the surface any jumbled thoughts or feelings

4.2   Developing an understanding of one's own personal style through regular practice

4.3   Stimulate personal creativity

4.4   Discovering opportunities to: -

4.4.1   Explore new topics

4.4.2   Generate fresh ideas

4.4.3   Build upon present writing skills

4.4.4   Exposes any weaknesses in style and grammar

4.4.5   Try out a variety of writing styles

Section 5: Ways to Improve Writing Style

Ways to improve writing style include: -

5.1   Simply enjoying the art of writing for its own sake

5.2   Welcoming it as part of everyday life

5.3   Keeping a daily journal to record new ideas

5.4   Creatively imitating the style of great authors or thinkers, without falling into the trap of plagiarism

5.5   Employing imagery when teasing out the meaning of difficult words or concepts *e.g. "To understand the Second Law of Thermodynamics it's helpful to imagine a sandcastle being blown away by the wind."*

5.6   Gaining the help of an editor to pinpoint strengths and weaknesses in a personal style

5.7   Constructively criticising one's own use of the English language when editing

5.8   Welcoming (and acting upon) constructive criticism from others

5.9   Participating in a *'writers' group'*

5.10   Highlighting exceptionally good or exceptionally poor words and phrases

5.11   Reading (aloud) a piece of written work to oneself and then asking *"Does this read well?"*

5.12   Telling the *'story'* – as if writing to a friend

5.13   Briefly summarising the main points

5.14   Practising the art of writing in: -

5.14.1   Answers to questions

5.14.2   Articles

5.14.3   Descriptions

5.14.4   Dialogues

5.14.5   Letters

5.14.6   Newspaper reports

5.14.7   Personal accounts

5.14.8   Poems

5.14.9   Stories

5.14.10 Summaries

The best way to improve writing style is unceasing practice. As most writers tend to be blind to their own faults, they would be strongly advised to obtain external feedback from those willing to give objective criticism. These may either be professional proof-readers and editors or more rarely, family and friends. However, the writer concerned must be able to accept the criticism that's being offered. If they're unwilling to do so, the quality of their writing will suffer and they could embarrass themselves by making silly mistakes.

Section 6: Closing Comments

Appendix 1 shows that, by acting as a basis for a significant number of new ideas, *'free writing'* (along with background *'planning'* and *'research'*) can mark the effective beginning (the first stage) of a written piece of work.

Appendix 1:
The Stages of Producing a Written Work

Stage 1: Preliminary Activities

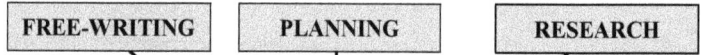

FREE-WRITING	PLANNING	RESEARCH

Stage 2: Putting Together
(May need the help of a proof-reader)

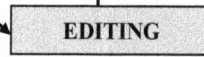

EDITING

Stage 3: Writing Out
(Continue drafting until it reads well)

DRAFTING

COMPLETION

STUDY AID 6: ASSIGNMENT PLANNING

Contents

AIMS

SECTION 1: Opening comments

SECTION 2: Types of Assignments

SECTION 3: Types of Essay

SECTION 4: The purpose of an Assignment

SECTION 5: Subject selection

SECTION 6: Title selection

SECTION 7: Planning an Assignment

SECTION 8: Completed planning notes

SECTION 9: Readership

SECTION 10: Levels of readership

SECTION 11: Essay and report writing

SECTION 12: Stages in report writing

SECTION 13: Plagiarism

SECTION 14: Closing comments

Aims

The study skills learnt in this section should enable the student to: -

- Plan a written assignment

- Understand the different types of assignment

- Select a pertinent title

- Consider the reader's needs and wishes

- Pick out the differences between essay and report writing

- Avoid plagiarism

- Organise his/her work effectively

Section 1: Opening Comments

An **Assignment** is any oral, practical or written task given to a student with a view to assessing his/her competence in a subject area. It can include anything from set essays and reports through to verbal presentations in class. **Assignment skills** are those which the student uses to produce the highest possible marks for which their subject knowledge allows.

One type of assignment is an **essay**, which is a written attempt to describe facts and to logically put forward a case, using any available evidence. Usually confined to one subject, it derives from the French word *'essayer'* meaning *'to attempt.'* When preparing an essay its best to be aware that most readers follow a set order of interest, which is: -

1.1   Themselves first

1.2   Other people next

1.3   Things affecting themselves next

1.4   Things affecting other people next

1.5   Abstract concepts last

In terms of their content and style essays range from the very straightforward to the very complicated and appeal to readers at different levels of education.

Section 2: Types of Assignments

Types of Assignment are: -

2.1   ORAL, *i.e.*

2.1.1   An individual presentation

2.1.2   A group presentation

2.1.3   A formal speech

Any one of the above may include answering questions put forward by an audience

2.2   WRITTEN, *i.e.*

2.2.1   A formal exam

2.2.2   A Research Report

2.2.3   A short or long essay (often called a Dissertation)

2.2.4   An academic Thesis

2.3   PRACTICAL, *i.e.*

2.3.1   Demonstrations with equipment

2.3.2   Preparing a display and sample of work

A *'practical'* assignment could mean almost anything and must remain within the bounds of *'health and safety.'*

Sometimes the title of an assignment may be *'set'* or *'negotiated'* – the latter decided upon after discussion with relevant education authorities. Each type of assignment places different pressures upon the student.

A *'set assignment'* tends to offer a clear structure which the student then follows. However, this advantage is quickly countered by its rigidity which may demand proficiency in areas in which the student feels less able. By way of contrast, a *'negotiated assignment'* offers the student a chance to explore areas in which they have a genuine interest. However, this benefit may again be countered by constraints made upon time and resources. This, in turn, may force the student to impose severe modifications upon any original ideas.

Section 3: Types of Essay

Types of essay are: -

3.1   <u>**Discursive**</u> – where the writer <u>agrees</u> or <u>disagrees</u> with various interpretations of an event. Either of the chosen viewpoints must be supported by valid reasons.

3.2   <u>**Evaluatory**</u> **(judgmental)** – where an explanation is given concerning <u>why</u> certain events took place

3.3   <u>**Factual**</u> – where as accurate a description as possible is given concerning <u>what</u> happened

3.4   <u>**Mixed**</u> – combining most (or all) of the above **(3.1-3.3)**

At higher educational levels, essays tend to become more evaluative than factual. This means that: -

- At **GCSE** level essays are mainly *'factual'* – at **'A'** level they're mainly mixed

- At undergraduate and postgraduate level, they're mainly *'evaluative'* (although longer essays tend to be *'mixed'* again).

Section 4: The Purpose of Assignments

The purpose of Assignments (including written essays) is to: -

4.1   Encourage research into, and reflection upon, a specific subject

4.2   Pick out any gaps in the student's knowledge

4.3   Increase knowledge and aid the learning process

4.4   Present a well-structured case

4.5   Develop a greater understanding of the subject

4.6   Assess the student's progress in a subject

4.7   Clarify the student's opinion on a subject

4.8   Strengthen self-expression

4.9   Provide useful work skills, *e.g.* report writing

Section 5: Subject Selection

When selecting a subject (or topic) the student is often faced with many options – especially in larger projects a subject should be selected which: -

5.1   Is interesting

5.2   Will gain the approval of the relevant education authorities

5.3   Will provide much research material

5.4   Will nurture the student's professional skills.

In selecting a subject, the second and third criteria must have priority over the other two – *e.g.* it would be a waste of time to choose a fascinating subject only to find that there wasn't enough research material for it. Also, try avoiding a subject which may prove extremely tedious.

Section 6: Title Selection

A *'Title'* aids the general emphasis of an assignment and should be: -

6.1   Brief

6.2   Eye-catching

6.3   Informative

6.4   Memorable

6.5   A description of *'the essence'* of the Assignment

6.6   An original *'building block'* upon which to write possible future essays

Always <u>keep to the subject of the Title,</u> *i.e.* if it's *'Sunflowers in the Caucasus'* then the student should write about this and not wander off to describe *'Tulips in Holland!'*

Section 7: Planning an Assignment

Good planning is the mother of good writing. When preparing an essay (or some other form of assignment) the first questions to ask are: *"<u>Why</u> am I writing this?"* and *"<u>Who</u> am I writing it for?"* Planning can be sub-divided into the following stages: -

Stage 1: Outline Plan

The *'outline plan'* must be clear, concise and consistent. It should: -

1.1   Decide for whom the essay is being written (its *'readership'*)

1.2   Explain the central purpose of the essay

Stage 2: Creation

Ideas are best generated through: -

2.1   *'THOUGHT SHOWERS'* – noting ideas down in random order

2.2   **WORD ASSOCIATION** – selecting a *'key'* (important) word from the Title and writing any words associated with it. A *'spider diagram'* would show each separate idea (see **p.24** for a diagrammatic representation)

2.3   **RESEARCH** – obtaining sufficient information to complete the assignment

2.4   **SEQUENTIAL NOTE-TAKING** – placing ideas into list order with the aid of bullet points

Stage 3: Organisation:

Ideas are placed into a *'rough and ready'* order by: -

3.1   Discarding all unhelpful material

3.2   Separating the remaining ideas into a **beginning, middle** and **end**

Stage 4: Development:

The essay is given further substance through: -

4.1   The gathering of more primary and/or secondary research

4.2   The development of existing ideas and the generation of new ones (if any)

Stage 5: Formulation:

Key elements must be included by: -

5.1   Drawing up a detailed plan – with the information and arguments placed in the order in which they'll be written in the main body of the essay

5.2   Noting (or highlighting) those essential words and phrases which must to be included

Stage 6: Drafting:

A first draft outline is written then subsequently corrected or amended. This process is repeated for if it takes to reach a competent, readable (and factually correct) *'final draft'* which is the preamble to the finished product.

Sometimes students are encouraged to employ the *'three say technique'* in relation to essay planning.

SAY   what you're going to say *e.g. "This essay will argue against Capital Punishment."*

SAY   it *e.g. "Capital Punishment is wrong because..."*

SAY   that you've said it *"Having argued against Capital Punishment it's reasonable to conclude that the arguments against it are stronger than those for it."*

The *'three say'* technique is especially helpful for beginners (or when writing rough drafts). It's most useful in the initial *'free writing'* stage of an essay.

Section 8: Completed Planning Notes

When all planning stages have been completed the following should be kept for reference purposes: -

8.1 *'Thought shower'* notes (often in the form of *'Spider Diagrams'*)

8.2 Lists of all electronic and non-electronic information sources

8.3 Planning notes, with a timetable of days/dates for <u>when</u> tasks need to be completed

8.4 Sequential notes – showing listed material gained from primary or secondary research

All the above are best placed in separate sections and filed away for easy access.

Section 9: Readership

One important consideration is, *"For whom am I writing this essay?"* The audience may be: -

9.1 **Homogeneous** – comprising of a similar <u>type of person</u> *e.g.* **'A'** Level Examiners

9.2 **Heterogeneous** – comprising of a <u>diversity of people</u> *e.g.* employees, examiners and fellow students

Another related consideration is *"In what frame of mind is the audience likely to be?"* An over-worked examiner with a hundred other essays to mark is likely to have far less patience than a fellow expert with the whole of the summer break to reflect upon your essay. Make it as concise and as clear as possible.

Section 10: Levels of Readership

A further factor to consider is *"At what level (or grade) are the readers operating?"* Here, the reader can either be:

10.1 **Higher** – those possessing a sophisticated knowledge within a given subject area *e.g.* employer, examiner or specialist

10.2 **Intermediate** – those possessing equal knowledge of a given subject area *e.g.* fellow employees and students

10.3 **Foundational** – those possessing less knowledge in each subject area *e.g.* business clients, juniors, students, or anyone under authority.

Section 11: Essay and Report Writing

An Essay differs from a Report in the following ways: -

	Essay	**Report**
11.1	Answers a set Title or Question	The Title is often negotiated
11.2	Is designed to increase theoretical knowledge	Is designed to use theoretical knowledge to deal with some practical issues
11.3	Can be short or long	Is often long
11.4	Often follows a simple three-part structure, with a **beginning, middle** and an end	Tends to follow a several-part structure with chapter and/or section headings
11.5	Is sometimes written in a literary style	Is normally written in a factual, analytical style
11.6	Its main content is centred upon '*text book*' knowledge	Its main content is taken from primary and secondary research data
11.7	Has very few or even no Footnotes or Appendices	Contains Footnotes and Appendices

By nature, a Report tests a far wider skill-range than an Essay. The Report requires a working knowledge of the subject, sound writing ability and a talent for organisation. Whilst it's usually true to say that a bad essay writer is almost always a bad report writer, this does not mean that a good essay writer is always a good report writer. To succeed, a report writer needs other contributory characteristics *i.e.* the ability to plough through what can often be very frustrating research material.

Section 12: Stages in Report Writing

Report writing involves the following, often overlapping stages: -

12.1 Collecting relevant facts from electronic and non-electronic sources

12.2 Uncovering what those facts reveal

12.3 Putting forward a reasoned statement based upon the available evidence

Section 13: Plagiarism

Before beginning a written assignment <u>it's essential</u> to become familiar with the term *'plagiarism.'* It means <u>the use of someone else's ideas and words without acknowledging them.</u> Material belonging to someone else is claimed as one's own. This is blatant theft of another person's (or organization's) work and is the deadliest of all sins in the academic world.

Plagiarism <u>can often be spotted</u> because the writer's own style doesn't *'match'* that of the source. It can be prevented by: -

13.1 Having a justified confidence in one's own knowledge and writing style

13.2 Expressing other people's ideas in one's own words whilst citing the original source *e.g.* one argument against government economic policy was that it had led to the creation of an unsustainably large Public Sector *(D. B. Smith 2011).*

13.3 Making a careful note of any references and source material which need to be quoted or cited

13.4 Placing any quotes within quotation marks

13.5 Citing a source, either with or without brackets *e.g. 'Bagnall suggested'* Or *'Per one viewpoint (T. Bagnall 1996).'* Where possible, such citations should include the year in which the source was first published.

Copyright Violation takes place when there's an unauthorised replication of someone else's literature by either electronic or non-electronic means. Penalties can be extremely severe as it's regarded as a form of intellectual theft. It often occurs in conjunction with Plagiarism.

Up to date information on the laws regarding Plagiarism and Copyright Violation are found in the latest edition of *'The Artist and Writer's Handbook,'* available in most public and academic libraries. Readers are <u>strongly advised</u> to consult with this source and with their academic providers about this issue. (Academic providers should also be consulted as to which Harvard referencing system needs to be employed when citing or quoting the work of other parties.)

A fuller and more technical discussion of issues pertaining to Plagiarism will be found in the *'Additional Note'* on **p.186**. This will outline the different levels of Plagiarism before giving practical suggestions that will help students to avoid it.

Section 14: Closing Comments

Careful and adequate preparation can save much unnecessary work in the later stages of assignment writing, with less drafts being needed to finish the work. Also, it's best to keep as close to the main point of the Title as possible. <u>The writer should always aim to stimulate (and not irritate) the reader. Examiners are often very tired people, labouring under a lot of pressure.</u> Good writing is likely to please them and gain extra marks.

At all levels of education, good communication is crucially important. Ideally, the student should aim to write for the intelligent person in the street.

STUDY AID 7: INTRODUCTIONS

Contents

AIMS

SECTION 1: Opening comments

SECTION 2: Types of Introduction

SECTION 3: Effective Introductions

SECTION 4: Ways to kill a good Introduction

SECTION 5: Introducing arguments

SECTION 6: Closing comments

Aims

The study skills learnt in this section should enable the student to: -

- Understand the role of Introductions

- Write effective Introductions

- Introduce arguments

- Gain the reader's attention

Section 1: Opening Comments

An introduction is a paragraph that marks the beginning of a written assignment. In an essay, it often consists of one opening paragraph, whilst in a larger work it merits a separate section (of a few or many paragraphs) of its own.

Its main role is to: -

1.1   Define key terms

1.2   Give reasons as to why a subject is being addressed

1.3   Outline any unavoidable limitations to the present written work

1.4   Clearly put forward the main subject (as distinct from subsidiary subjects)

1.5   State any key assumptions or prejudices

1.6   Acknowledge and thank outside help given. In a larger work this may require its own separate section, entitled *'Acknowledgements'*.

Section 2: Types of Introduction

Types of Introduction include: -

2.1   An *'Executive Summary'* which places all the main points together

2.2   A *'Foreword'* which introduces someone else's work

2.3   A list of *'Key Definitions'* (especially in technical subjects)

2.4   A *'Preface'* containing personal comments about how the work was produced

2.5   A *'Synopsis'* – giving a brief outline of the whole work

2.6   Personal dedications to family, friends or colleagues

2.7   An additional *'Acknowledgements'* section (see **1.6** above)

Section 3: Effective Introductions

To write an effective Introduction, the writer should: -

3.1   Link it directly to the Title

3.2   Allow it to *'set the scene'* for the rest of the work

3.3   Make it as concise as possible

3.4   Attempt to create a favourable impression

3.5   Distinguish (set it apart) from the **main body** of the assignment – often achieved by simply inserting a missed line

3.6   Give the clear impression that the subject in hand has been understood

3.7   Entice the audience to read further by: -

3.7.1   Making use of a startling quote or an interesting expression, *e.g. "The clock struck thirteen"* which began George Orwell's novel 1984

3.7.2   Employing a topical sentence, *e.g. "This essay will examine the topic of crime in the North of England."*

3.7.3   Striking a note of controversy*, e.g. "This polemical article defends destroys the ridiculous myth that ..."*

When preparing a first draft it's often helpful to write out the **main body** of an assignment and its **conclusion** before writing out the **Introduction.**   This ensures that, when the Introduction is finally written, it should flow naturally from the thoughts and ideas already accumulated in the writer's head.

Section 4: Ways to Kill a Good Introduction

4.   Ways to *'kill'* a good Introduction are: -

4.1   Not to have one at all!

4.2   Portrayal a vague, lack-lustre stance

4.3   Cramming far too much of the **main body** into it

4.4   Not relating it to: -

4.4.1   The main Question or Title

4.4.2   The **main body** or **Conclusion**

4.5   Taking an apologetic stance which emphasise what has not accomplished in each piece of work. (This simply places shortcomings in the glare of unwanted publicity.)

Section 5: Introducing Arguments

A short sentence introduces a specific argument which: -

5.1   Immediately attracts the reader's attention

5.2   Directs the reader's train of thought

5.3   Prepares the way for further supporting evidence

5.4   Sums up the central theme

Sometimes such argumentation can be used to stir-up controversy on matters about which people hold very strong opinions, *e.g. "It's reasonable to argue that Karl Marx's real motive was a spiteful lust for power."*

Section 6: Closing Comments

A good Introduction is important in creating a favourable impression and in *'setting the scene'* for what is to follow. it distinctly precedes the *'main body,'* whilst simultaneously leading naturally toward it.

STUDY AID 8: ARGUING SKILLS

Contents

AIMS

SECTION 1: Opening comments

SECTION 2: Essay conventions

SECTION 3: Prioritisation

SECTION 4: Effective argumentation

SECTION 5: Characteristics of a good argument

SECTION 6: Closing an argument

SECTION 7: Grouping causes

SECTION 8: The advantages of causal groupings

SECTION 9: Figures and diagrams

SECTION 10: Closing comments

Aims

The study skills learnt in this section should enable the student to: -

- Follow essay conventions

- Sift relevant from irrelevant information

- Retain control over the middle part of the essay

- Present effective arguments

- Place an analysis of causes into neat categories

- Further illustrate an argument (if needed) with legible figures and diagrams

- Close an argument

Section 1: Opening Comments

Arguing skills are those which present evidence-based viewpoints in an orderly, logical and plausible manner. They're often placed within the *'main body'* of the essay and strive to: -

1.1   Keep to the original aims of the essay

1.2   Sift relevant from irrelevant information

1.3   Present an orderly *'list'* of causes, based upon verifiable data and views *'for and against'* an argument or research finding

Section 2: Essay Conventions

Essay Conventions are those guidelines which must be followed if a written piece of work is to score high marks. Using them makes the art of reading and writing far more enjoyable. They consist of: -

A Citation – an indirect description of an argument which uses *'reported speech'* to reference another person's work *e.g. 'Professor Jones criticised Professor Smith's theory for its lack of scientific validity.'*

A Paraphrase (or summary of a quote) which must be clearly distinguished from both a direct quotation and a citation, e.g. *'According to Professor Hyde the speed of light is a universal constant.'*

An Amplification, brings out a fuller meaning of a word and should be placed in brackets ( ) as should dates, citations and brief numerical information *e.g. "The speed of light is a universal constant (its speed cannot vary in any part of the universe)," * (Hyde 2012).

A Quotation – is a direct insertion of another person's work. **Short quotations** (usually those under thirty words) are enclosed in quotation marks *e.g.* Professor Jones said *"Professor Smith's theory lacks scientific validity."* However, **long quotations** should be printed in single typescript as a separate paragraph (which is sometimes indented to the left for clarification), *e.g.* Richard Smith (2011) in the preface to his poetry book *'At 47'* revealed that: -

> *"A key characteristic of this collection is the variability in both style and subject matter. In **Part A,** especially, readers just do not know what is coming next. A happy go-lucky poem about a pussycat could easily be followed by something abstract on Post Modernism; a sad poem involving death could be followed by a biting satire on some aspect of Britain's contemporary political and social scene. A conscious attempt has been made to explore a wide range of human emotions and topics."*

Lines of poetry or verse are usually distinguished by a diagonal line (/) as in the case of one of the poems in *'At 47,' e.g. "At forty-seven/I discovered/I was a Poet/Didn't want it! / Didn't expect it!"*

Quotations serve to: -

2.1   Convey the flavour of a work

2.2   Illustrate the point being made

2.3   Provide a source for information or analysis

2.4   Succinctly express a thought or concept

Quotes within a quote can be distinguished by single quotation marks, *e.g.* whilst driving he remarked to his wife, *"This is the road my friend said would 'definitely lead' to our destination. I hope he's right."*

It's essential to acknowledge another person's work when making use of it, no matter whether it's a quote, citation or paraphrase. Failure to do so could open one up to the charge of plagiarism (illegally stealing another person's work, see **p.72**).

Section 3: Prioritisation

Prioritisation is of the utmost importance in the **main body** of an essay. Material must be sifted through to find out what: -

3.1   Must be used

3.2   May be used (if time allows)

3.3   Must not be used

Some points will require in-depth whilst others will need mentioning only briefly.

Section 4: Effective Argumentation

To argue effectively it's best to: -

4.1   Gain the reader's attention by beginning with a pertinent point or comment

4.2   Place the points into groupings, (*e.g.* arguments *'for'* and *'against'*)

4.3   Ensure each sentence *'flows naturally'* from its predecessor

4.4   Keep each section of the argument within the size of one paragraph

4.5   Make effective use of: -

4.5.1 Coherent logic

4.5.2 Recognised authorities

4.5.3 Relevant supporting evidence

Section 5: Characteristics of a Good Argument

A well-thought-out argument must: -

5.1   Be supported by a variety of factual evidences, taken directly from different sources

5.2   Gain the reader's sympathy and emotional support

5.3   Avoid criticising alternative viewpoints from a position of ignorance

5.4   Understand and articulate alternative viewpoints

5.5   Possess a logical coherence

5.6   Be objective (describe how things are)

5.7   Be clearly summarised

5.8   Be open to new insights

5.9   Be open to verification

5.10   Be precise and orderly

5.11   Be willing to acknowledge that it could be wrong

5.12   Avoid giving way to flimsy rhetoric or superficial pomposity

5.13   Ignore any unfounded vilification (accusing insults and personal attacks)

Section 6: Closing an Argument

To bring an argument to its close the writer should: -

6.1   State briefly whether he/she is *'for'*, *'against'*, *'neutral'* or *'undecided'*

6.2   State briefly the reasons <u>why</u> a certain stance is being taken

6.3   Use a brief, pertinent and decisive sentence to close matters *"After weighing all the evidence carefully a resounding 'no' must be given to the question posed in the title."*

Section 7: Grouping Causes

When attempting an essay the writer is often asked <u>why</u> something happened *e.g. 'Why did the Russian Revolution take place in 1917?'* This means that relevant causes need to be placed into certain groupings. Examples of such groupings are: -

7.1 Order of Importance: Beginning with the most (or least) important causes first, then moving along to those least (or more) important next.   Although logical, this order presupposes that the writer is already able to distinguish the *'more'* from the *'less'* important causes.

7.2 Order of Subject Area: Dividing the causes into neat categories, *i.e.* *'economic'*, *'military*, *'political'* and *'social.'* Although such orderliness is useful in thematic studies, it does raise the question over which sub-division should come first, *e.g.* should the political causes of the Russian Revolution be placed before or after the economic ones?

7.2 Order of Time: Beginning with the more recent causes first, then moving on to those more distant in time. (Conversely, the writer could begin with the more distant causes first before moving on to the more recent ones.) This approach enables the writer to refrain from lurching about on a time-scale. A short-term cause would be the outbreak of World War One in 1914; whilst a middle-term would be the Accession of Tsar Nicholas the Second in 1894: and finally, a long-term cause would be the development of a revolutionary tradition since Napoleon's defeat in 1814. However, this approach does pre-suppose a good grasp of chronology, which may or may not be the case.

The writer would need to distinguish clearly between the short, middle and long-term causes. In relation to the Russian Revolution, it's possible to place its causes in the following order: -

- Most important: military (short, middle and long term)

- Next most important: economic (short, middle and long term)

- Least important: political (short, middle and long term)

Section 8: The Advantages of Causal Groupings

Causes placed in a certain logical order have the advantage of: -

8.1   Permitting the reader to follow a steady train of thought

8.2   Providing a structure for the main body of the assignment

8.3   Preventing a hasty *'scrambling about'* from one point to another

8.4   Lessening the chance of inserting irrelevant information

Section 9: Figures and Diagrams

If a figure or diagram is to be inserted into a written piece of work, then a clear order should be followed: -

9.1   A brief *'introductory sentence'* to the figure (or diagram), stating its relevance within the work

9.2   The figure (or diagram) itself – neatly presented with only the necessary amount of detail

9.3   A brief commentary on what the figure (diagram) means and its wider implications

To produce a figure (or diagram) without either introducing or commenting upon it would not be acceptable. In long assignments figures/diagrams are best inserted in the appendices – otherwise they could break the flow of the narrative. However, at certain times inserting a figure/diagram in the main body of the essay may aid understanding; whether to do so lies wholly at the discretion of the writer.

Section 10: Closing Comments

The **main body** is that part of the essay where it's easiest to lose control, especially when arguing *'for or against'* something. Ever present is the constant danger of wandering from the central focus and of losing marks for including irrelevant material. To prevent this situation from arising, a careful application of the writing skills described in **Study Aid 4** is needed. Regular reference to the question should also help to keep the essay smoothing smoothly as it should.

STUDY AID 9: PARAGRAPHS

Contents

AIMS

SECTION 1: Opening comments

SECTION 2: Paragraph openings

SECTION 3: Structural features

SECTION 4: Stylistic features

SECTION 5: Paragraph endings

SECTION 6: The advantages (and disadvantages) of brief sentences

SECTION 7: The advantages (and disadvantages) of long sentences

SECTION 8: Punctuation

SECTION 9: Closing Comments

Aims

The study skills learnt in this section should enable the student to: -

- Write gripping paragraph openings

- Control the *'direction'* of the paragraph

- Employ brief (as well as long) sentences

- Punctuate the work accordingly

- Make the work comprehensible to outside parties

- Close paragraphs in a brisk, business-like manner

Section 1: Opening Comments

A sentence consists of a meaningful collection of words, centred upon one specific point. A paragraph consists of a collection of sentences all focused upon one main theme or topic.

Sentences and paragraphs serve to: -

1.1   Break down a piece of writing into its constituent parts

1.2   Show how informative points and arguments relate to one another

1.3   Guide the reader's train of thought

Section 2: Paragraph Openings

When a paragraph is *'opened'* it should: -

2.1   Begin by saying things the reader understands or probably expects to hear

2.2   Contain an opening sentence which: -

2.2.1   Relate to the Essay Title (or Sub-Titles of a larger assignment)

2.2.2   Convey the issues at hand

2.2.3   Captivate the reader's attention

2.2.4   Be brief and to the point

2.2.5   Clearly introduce the main point or argument

2.2.6   Be relatively uncomplicated

Section 3: Structural Features

A well-written paragraph is characterised by: -

3.1   A clear focus upon one topic

3.2   A natural *"linking up"* with previous and succeeding paragraphs

3.3   A style that is appropriate, brief, direct, lucid, simple and vigorous

3.4   A suitable sentence structure, beginning with: -

3.4.1   An indented, short *'opening'* sentence – pointing directly to the topic and providing any needed explanation

3.4.2   A more detailed *'middle'* sentence area – enlarging upon explanations, proffering logical arguments and providing factual support

3.4.3   A short *'closing'* sentence to round everything off

3.5   A good paragraph should ensure that each sentence: -

3.5.1   Expresses one main thought related to the theme or topic being covered

3.5.2   Keeps to one theme or topic

3.6   The *'short-long short'* (SLS) sequence should be used throughout a paragraph, *i.e.*

3.6.1   A shorter sentence at the beginning

3.6.2   Longer sentences in the middle

3.6.3   A shorter sentence at the end

3.7   A line space must be placed between each paragraph

Of importance is the *'short-long-short'* sequence. Failure to follow this results in a paragraph woefully lacking in structure. Using over-long sentences creates a rambling paragraph that leaves the reader thinking *"What was that I just read – somehow it seemed vague and unclear?"* Information provided at the beginning of the sentence will have been largely forgotten by its end. In contrast, using only short sentences creates a very abrupt paragraph with so many brief points that the reader is left thinking *"There's too much to take in here."* The SLS sequence is an excellent tool to prevent such problems from arising.

Section 4: Stylistic Features

In terms of content and style a well-written paragraph is characterised by: -

4.1   Being lucid and easy to read

4.2   Following a carefully structured plan

4.3   Containing emphatic (strong) opening and closing sentences, each directing the reader's attention to the topic in hand

4.4   Conveying useful information in a clear and understandable way

4.5   Ensuring that <u>every sentence</u> is relevant to the main theme

4.6   Ensuring that the sentences flow in logical stages – so carrying the argument forward

4.7   Excluding unnecessary flamboyance (exaggeration) in writing style

4.8   Excluding complex diagrams and tables – these should ideally be placed in Appendices – especially in long pieces of work

4.9   <u>Not</u> venturing to make any new points unless they can be adequately developed

4.10 Resisting the temptation to over labour a point

4.11 Revealing where the writer stands in relation to any argument (whether *'for,'* *'against'* or *'neutral'*)

4.12 Showing a respectful attitude toward its readership by <u>not</u> telling them what they should or should not think

Section 5: Paragraph Endings

When a paragraph is closed, it should: -

5.1   Briefly summarise the main point(s) already put forward in the paragraph

5.2   Round everything off with a short sentence, bringing the focus to a definite close

5.3   Briefly introduce the topic to be found in the next paragraph

5.4   Resolve any remaining confusion that may still linger in the reader's mind

5.5   Avoid finishing either too abruptly or in a meandering manner

Section 6:
The Advantages (and Disadvantages) of Brief Sentences

	Advantages: Brief Sentences can:	Disadvantages: Brief Sentences can:
6.1	Be easy to read	Hinder detailed argument
6.2	Offer a useful step in an argument	Appear dogmatic and superficial
6.3	Provide clear introductions and endings	Be abrupt and tedious if overused
6.4	Use *'punchy quotations'* – which remain in the reader's mind	

Section 7:
The Advantages (and Disadvantages) of Long Sentences

	Advantages: Long Sentences can:	Disadvantages: Long Sentences can:
7.1	Add extra information and detail	Be long-winded
7.2	Cause the reader to pause and think	Weaken the basic structure in a paragraph
7.3	Develop and further qualify a point	Bore the reader
7.4	Give scope for rhetorical flourishes	Cause the reader to forget the information given in the first part of the sentence

Ideally, no sentence should have more than fifteen words before a comma, full stop or some other form of punctuation. This enables the reader to pause and assimilate what's been read.

Section 8: Punctuation

Basic punctuation is an absolute necessity for effective paragraphing. Common punctuation symbols are: -

8.1 **FULL STOPS (.)** These separate sentences.

8.2 **COLONS (:)** These can be interpreted to mean *'as follows'.* They usually precede lists or long quotations. After a full stop, they constitute the second strongest break in a sentence.

8.3 **SEMI-COLONS (;)** link-up two closely related parts which would sound disjointed if placed into two separate sentences. Usually, the second clause explains or qualifies the first. For example: *"He was dying slowly and in great pain; for he had caught a virus when exploring the Amazon Basin."*

8.4 **COMMAS (,)** are often used to replace the word *'and;'* they break up a sentence into its constituent parts, providing a useful break for the reader. They can also divide lists into meaningful sections, *e.g. "At the local shop, she purchased apples, bananas, pears and oranges."*

8.5   **DASHES (–)** are used to denote a pause or to provide extra supplementary information. They're often used toward the end of a sentence. For example: *"The wheels of the upturned vehicle kept turning slowly – making a low whirring sound."* They are longer than hyphens and have a space either side of them.

8.6   **HYPHENS (-)** are used to divide hyphenated surnames or words that run together *i.e. 'The Lock-up.'* Unlike dashes, hyphens are shorter lines with NO space either side of them. For example: *"The new boy's name was Harding-Cox."*

8.7   **CURVED BRACKETS ( )** are used to insert supplementary information, *i.e.* citations and alternative meanings or phrases. Their function is to preserve the flow of words or individual thoughts. They're placed within or at the end of a sentence. For example: *"When the First World War (known also as the Great War) broke out (in August 1914) a new era had begun, (Smith 1989)"*

8.8   **SQUARE BRACKETS [ ]** are used to insert clarifying words, phrases or comments not found in the original text, whilst preserving the flow of words or individual thoughts. They're placed anywhere within the sentence.   One example is the Amplified Bible's Version of Ephesians 2:14 which highlights the distinctive function of both curved and squared brackets: - *"For He is [Himself] our peace – our bond of unity and harmony. He has made us both [Jew and Gentile] one (body) and has broken down (destroyed, abolished) the hostile dividing wall between us."*

8.9   **INDENTED SQUARE BRACKETS (also known as CURLY BRACKETS) { }** are used to separate the different parts of a mathematical formula to aid calculation and make it more easily understood. For example: $\{a+ b/c\} – \{xy/z^2\}$. They're often used in computer programming. (However curved brackets are often used in their place.)

8.10   **DOUBLE INVERTED COMMAS** Begin and end a speech quotation – enclosing spoken words. For example, I shouted, *"To be or not to be, that is the question."*

8.11   **SINGLE INVERTED COMMAS** Often used interchangeably with **8.7**, also denoting thoughts or quotes within quotes. For example, *"Mark Anthony said 'and Brutus was an honourable man,' with great sarcasm."* They may also be used to highlight a word to draw the reader's attention to it as with *'and'* in **8.4**.

8.12   **QUESTION MARKS (?)** These simply denote the end of a question, *e.g. "what was his name?"*

8.13   **EXCLAMATION MARKS (!)** These denote surprise, or an emphatic statement, *e.g. "Oh no!"*

Section 9: Closing Comments

Good sentence and paragraph structure provide a solid foundation for effective writing. They make the content of any written work comprehensible to the reader.

STUDY AID 10: CONCLUSIONS

Contents

AIMS

SECTION 1: Opening comments

SECTION 2: Types of Conclusion

SECTION 3: Characteristics of a good conclusion

SECTION 4: Improving conclusions

SECTION 5: Addenda

SECTION 6: Appendices

SECTION 7: Footnotes

SECTION 8: Bibliographies

SECTION 9: Overall structure of Bibliographies

SECTION 10: Closing comments

APPENDICES

APPENDIX 1:   Overview of an effective Assignment/Essay structure

Aims

The study skills learnt in this section should enable the student to: -

- Know what type of Conclusion to write

- Write a clear Conclusion related to the Assignment

- Draw up a well-structured *'Addendum'*

- Understand the purpose of Appendices and Footnotes

- Design useful Bibliographies

- Categorise the types of *'sources'* that go into a Bibliography

- Leave a good impression at the end of a given Assignment

Section 1: Opening Comments

Conclusions represent the final portion of a written Essay (or Assignment) and serve to bring the piece of written work to an effective close. They consist, almost always, of a written statement of opinion.

Section 2: Types of Conclusion

There are many types of Conclusion, each tailored to what's been written in the main body of the work: -

2.1 **The Affirmative Conclusion** – agrees with and supports the main point(s) put forward in the Question or Title

2.2 **The Contentious Conclusion** – disagrees with the main point(s) put forward in the Question or Title

2.3 **The Mixed Conclusion** – agrees with some, but not all aspects of the Question or Title

2.4 **The Neutral Conclusion** – neither agrees nor disagrees with the points put forward in the Question or Title; it may simply sum up what's already been stated

2.5 **The Tentative Conclusion** – assesses the available evidence and remains undecided or gives only a hesitant endorsement of the main point(s) put forward in the Question or Title

Mixed and tentative conclusions are more suitable for the higher reaches of education. This is because a greater complexity in subject matter makes a decisive conclusion more difficult.

It's essential to give a brief justification when using any one of the above conclusions. For example, should a writer give an *'undecided'* conclusion over who murdered the Princes in the Tower he's obliged to say why this was so. It's only courteous to let the reader know the reasons for adopting a viewpoint.

Section 3: Characteristics of a Good Conclusion

A good conclusion: -

3.1 Relates to the Title and to what's been stated in the **main body** of the essay

3.2 Matches, but does not repeat the **Introduction** or **main body** *'ad verbatim'* (word for word)

3.3 Briefly sums up the available evidence

3.4 Conveys a clear sense of having reached a definite ending using a short and succinctly written final sentence

3.5 Engages the reader's attention by giving the impression that they alone are being addressed

3.6 Provokes enquiring thought and even controversy

3.7 Reveals areas where further research may be needed

A good conclusion <u>totally avoids</u>: -

3.8 Meandering aimlessly to a close

3.9 Making dogmatic assertions, not based upon the evidence

3.10 Repeating in detail what's been said in the main body

3.11 Suddenly introducing a completely new topic

Section 4: Improving Conclusions

To reach a sound conclusion and to provide even greater clarity it would prove wise to include: -

4.1 A brief justification – providing valid reasons for coming to that conclusion. This should engage the examiner, making him aware that the subject was well understood.

4.2 Something which may be deemed as contentious. This is perfectly acceptable if it's pertinent and well-reasoned. This could score higher marks than a partially reasoned affirmative conclusion. (The examiner is not usually looking for *'yes men'*).

4.3 Factual (<u>not</u> dogmatic) assertions *e.g. "All Yorkshire men are mean"*

When it comes to writing a conclusion for an exam essay it's helpful to: -
- <u>Answer the question</u> that's been set
- <u>Justify that answer</u> with a brief, evidence based reason
- <u>Summarise that answer</u> with a short closing sentence

Section 5: Addenda

Addenda (from the Latin *'something added'* and the plural form of *'Addendum'*) give additional supporting evidence to the ideas put forward in the main body of a work. They're commonly found in academic works and include: -

5.1   Abstracts – these provide an introductory summary to an academic article or paper

5.2   Acknowledgements

5.3   Appendices

5.4   Charts, Diagrams, Tables and other visual material an introductory summary in the form of a numbered list

5.5   Descriptions of procedures

5.6   Executive Summaries which can provide a numbered list of key points

5.7   Glossaries (short explanations of key terms)

5.8   Bibliographies; these can be found in a variety of different formats *i.e.*

<u>Name and page number</u>
Jones A. 89, 146, 185
Jones B.   3, 14, 17
Karl C. 140, 150, 161, 178, 179

<u>Reference</u>
Genesis   3:16, 21, 24; 12:1-8, 20; 15:1 & 50:23f
(Chapters are separated by semi-colons and verses by commas. 50:23f means Genesis chapter fifty verse twenty-three to the finish.)
Exodus   20:1
Leviticus 17:11

<u>Subject</u> **(and page number where this subject is found)**
Meaning, 166-167. 189
Messiah, 467-468, 516,541,612, 777
Midrash, 3-4. 16-19. 20-21

Section 6: Appendices

Appendices serve to: -

6.1   Add further information relating to the main body either to amplify or to advance the main argument

6.2   Insert any last-minute developments, e.g. a new research finding

6.3   Give room for an interesting digression or description of a procedure

6.4   Present diagrams and statistical information

Section 7: Footnotes

Footnotes are shorter than Appendices and include that <u>extra</u> information which, if used in the main body, could well disrupt its flow. Whilst often sharing the same function as an Appendix, Footnotes also tend to:

7.1   Provide specific source references

7.2   Allow for personal comment, unacceptable elsewhere in the Assignment

7.3   Qualify or correct any factual errors

Footnotes may be placed either at the bottom of the page in which they are marked; at the end of individual chapters or at the end of a whole book. They are denoted in the work by an asterisk **(*)** number **(1)**, or a small letter **(a)**. Asterisks tend to be used when footnotes are relatively few in number and are then placed at the bottom of the relevant page. Overuse of asterisks can be distracting to the reader – its then better to use a number or a letter.

Section 8: Bibliographies

Ideally, Bibliographies should be presented in the following manner: -

8.1   Begin with the author's surname

8.2   Record the author's name and initials in reverse order e.g. Smith, R. J.

8.3   Insert the year of publication

8.4   Insert the main title and any sub-title of the work (this can be placed in *italics*)

8.5   Name the publisher

8.6   Record any **[ISBN]** or **[Library Reference]** numbers

All the above information should be well spaced and clearly visible to the reader, *e.g.*

Atwood Margaret (2010) *The Handmaid's Tale*, Vintage Classics, ISBN: 978-0099511663

Section 9: Overall Structure of Bibliographies

Long Bibliographies can be divided into: -

9.1   Book lists

9.2   Research papers

9.3   Other written documents

9.4   Media sources *e.g.* newspapers, radio and television

9.5   Other information sources *e.g.* personal interviews

Primary sources are to be clearly distinguished from secondary cries, *i.e.* the names of contributors to a survey should never be placed amongst the names of text book authors. (The only exception to this would be if they happened to be one and the same person.)

For non-exam essays a Bibliography is an absolute must; students are justly penalised should one be omitted. At the very least, a good Bibliography can help to refute any charge of plagiarism.

Section 10: Closing Comments

Good conclusions and helpful Addenda make for an effective essay or assignment, the main characteristics of which can be found in **Appendix 1.**

Appendix 1: Overview of an Effective Assignment/Essay Structure

Those Essays and Assignments which prove the most meaningful will contain: -

1.   An Introduction: this informs the reader of the main points being made and perhaps details of how it came to be written. It may (if in Report form) also contain a **Contents Page** and a **Glossary** of key terms. It provides a succinctly written summary containing a relevant selection of the following: -

1.1   The time-period being covered

1.2   A reiteration of the question – the answer to which will be found in the **main body** of the essay

1.3   A statement of the case about to be presented

1.4   An interesting hypothesis which will be tested and reported upon

1.5   An interesting quote which attracts the reader's attention and conveys ideas requiring further discussion in the main body of the essay

1.6   An outline of the reasons for adopting a focus or viewpoint

2.   A Main Body, wherein: -

2.1   Appropriate *'weighting'* (due care and attention) is given to the main points

2.2   Any irrelevancies are quickly discarded

2.3   Arguments are discussed in a logical manner

2.4   Different parts are linked together in a definite order

2.5   Full explanations (to answer the question posed) are offered

Each paragraph tackles one topic, theme or part of an argument. The paragraph itself is divided into an opening topic sentence, key discussion sentences and a closing summarising sentence.

3.   A **Conclusion,** which: -

3.1   Links naturally to the **Introduction**

3.2   Draws together and sums up the main points

3.3   Gives definite, practical recommendations

3.4   Provides a lucid and concise ending

3.5   Finishes the work with an evidence-based opinion

3.6   Suggests innovative ideas or points out areas requiring further research

4.   A **Structured Addendum,** which includes: -

4.1   Appendices

4.2   Footnotes

4.3   Bibliography

4.4   Index

(An **Addendum** tends to be used only for long Essays, Dissertations and Reports)

Glossaries and **Summaries (p.99)** are increasingly being placed at the beginning (rather than at the end) of a written piece of work. In business reports, Executive Summaries now usually come <u>before</u> any Introductory Comments.

STUDY AID 11: PROOF READING

Contents

AIMS

SECTION 1: Opening comments

SECTION 2: The stages of proof reading

SECTION 3: The advantages of proof reading aloud

SECTION 4: Things to look out for when proof reading

SECTION 5: Evaluating proof reading

SECTION 6: Clichés

SECTION 7: Closing comments

APPENDICES

APPENDIX 1: The relationship between the proof reading and essay drafting

Aims

The study skills learnt in this section should enable the student to: -

- Value the purpose of proof reading

- Proof read his/her own drafts

- Correct each mistake found in the draft

- Appreciate the advantages of proof reading aloud

- Assess the effectiveness of his/her proof reading

- Remove any clichés

- Realise that proof reading punctuates the process of drafting

Section 1: Opening Comments

Proof Reading is the process of reading through a written piece of work with the express intention of improving its quality. All manner of mistakes is removed or corrected, *i.e.* misspelt words, poor sentence construction and inappropriate punctuation. The result imparts the relevant information and reads well, thereby increasing the chances of gaining higher marks.

Section 2: The Stages of Proof Reading

Proof Reading often involves the following three stages: -

2.1   **Reading quickly through a piece of writing to check for: -**

2.1.1   Obvious errors

2.1.2   The general meaning

2.1.3   The general structure

2.1.4   Whether it adequately answers the question

2.2   **Reading it aloud two or three times to: -**

2.2.1   Assess whether the writing *'flows'* and makes sense

2.2.2   Uncover specific mistakes in wording and sentence structure

2.2.3   Make written corrections

2.3   **Reading it through again silently to: -**

2.3.1   Spot and correct remaining factual errors

2.3.2   Point out any remaining confusion

2.3.3   Check that all sources have been acknowledged

Ideally, each stage should be attempted on a separate day.

Section 3: The Advantages of Proof Reading Aloud

Reading a draft out loud can help to: -

3.1   Increase proficiency in the spoken language

3.2   Aid sentence flow

3.3   Focus attention upon words or phrases

3.4   Improve communication skills through practice

3.5   Provoke new thoughts and possible additions to the meaning of a sentence or word

3.6   Provide a sense of audience

Should a draft not make sense when read aloud then it's unlikely to make sense when read silently

Section 4: Things to Look Out for When Proof Reading

When reviewing a written piece of work, it's necessary to check whether: -

4.1   The **Introduction** and **Conclusion** are clearly distinguishable from the **main body** of writing

4.2   It links to the Title

4.3   A clear structure exists throughout the main body of writing

4.4   Diagrams and Statistical Tables are readily understood

4.5   Each mistake in grammar, punctuation and spelling is corrected

4.6   Appropriate evidence is used to justify (or refute) any stated argument

4.7   The facts used are correct

4.8   The essay *'flows'* from one point to the next – the sentences moving smoothly along without any stumbles or pauses

4.9   The causal explanations are *'grouped'* in an appropriate order

4.10 The given explanations and illustrations make sense

4.11 The important points are included and given enough attention

4.12 The paragraph divisions come in the right places, *i.e.* where the discussion or emphasis changes

4.13 The work is written in a style appropriate for the intended audience

4.14 The question is clearly answered

4.15 The right amount of evidence is given

4.16 Unnecessary words and phrases are deleted

4.17 Relevant sources are acknowledged, cited and quoted

Although it won't spot errors in grammatical structure, it can be especially helpful to proof read backwards to focus upon individual words and to reduce the risk of missing any mistakes. When checking through a piece of writing it pays to: -
- Speed-read a draft to gain familiarity with the general theme and to spot any structural problems
- Read the work backwards to look for missing or misspelt words
- Search through the work once or twice to remove any remaining mistakes

Ideally, each of the above stages should take place on different days and at a time when the mind is at its most fresh.

Section 5: Evaluating Proof Reading

After Proof Reading a piece of work it may be helpful to ask the following questions: -

5.1 What was the main purpose of this Assignment?

5.2 Has the material in the Assignment provided the basis for further research?

5.3 Have justified comments and criticisms (made by the proof-reader in previous drafts) been noted and acted upon?

5.4 Have relevant ideas been adequately expressed?

5.5 What could be changed if the Assignment was written again, and why?

5.6 Would anything of value be lost if words, sentences or paragraphs were deleted? (Remember, the examiner will not wish to read through unnecessary material)

Whilst proof reading, a whole variety of ideas and insights may well be gained – should these not be inserted in the present Assignment they must be noted down for future use elsewhere; they may well prove invaluable.

Section 6: Clichés

Proof Reading has an important function in getting rid of clichés. These are overused words and expressions which serve only to diminish the value of a written piece of work. Examples of clichés include: -

6.1 Acid test

6.2 An informed source

6.3 Achilles heel

6.4 Blue Sky thinking

6.5 Cart before the horse

6.6 Common sense will prevail

6.7 Fair and reasonable offer

6.8 In all cases

6.9 Informed opinion

6.10 It seems to me that

6.11 Liberation struggle

6.12 Literally

6.13 Moment of truth

6.14   Mounting crisis

6.15   The bare facts

6.16   The prevailing public mood

6.17   The sword of truth

6.18   Thin end of the wedge

6.19   Win-win situation

6.20   With regard and respect to

6.21   When and if (or *'if and when'*)

Clichés can be unknowingly picked up from the mass media – often creeping into the mind unawares only to resurface when writing. This is especially so when feeling fatigued or stressed.

Section 7: Closing Comments

7.1   Proof reading plays a vital part in the editing process

7.2   Proof reading tends to get easier with each successive draft, *i.e.* beginning with the **rough,** then the **provisional** and on to the **final** draft

7.3   As it requires a great deal of analytical skill, proof reading is best done at a time of the day when the reader is most mentally alert

7.4   Ideally, proof reading should punctuate the process of drafting **(Appendix 1)**

Great patience is required when proof reading and drafts can vary from the few to the many. It is often, by far, the most time-consuming activity in book publishing. When writing a book, it can be helpful (should time allow) to lay aside a manuscript for a few weeks (or even months) before attempting to correct it. What this does is to increase objectivity and provide a fresher mind to spot mistakes.

Appendix 1:
The Relationship Between Proof Reading and Essay Drafting

Rough Draft

↓   First Proof Read

Provisional Draft

↓   Second Proof Read

Final Draft

↓   Third Proof Read

Handing In

Proof reading involves checking for grammatical mistakes. It's not to be confused with content editing which involves checking for factual and citation errors. Many drafts may be needed to arrive at a well-written finished product. For published books, it's not unknown for there to be ten drafts between the beginnings of a project to its completion. The key to success is to keep on *'drafting'* until it reads correctly and well.

Proof Reading and Content Editing often constitutes the most arduous and time-consuming parts of the writing process – especially where Book Publishing is involved.

STUDY AID 12: EXAM SKILLS

Contents

AIMS

SECTION 1: Opening comments

SECTION 2: Qualities required

SECTION 3: Common reasons for failure in exam preparation

SECTION 4: More reasons for exam failure

SECTION 5: Exam preparation

SECTION 6: Approaching exam questions

SECTION 7: Time management

SECTION 8: Answering exam questions

SECTION 9: Structuring exam answers

SECTION 10: Closing comments

APPENDICES

APPENDIX 1: A list of *'instruction words'* used in exams

APPENDIX 2: *'A'* Level Grades

APPENDIX 3: *'Question Dissection'*

APENDIX 4: Planning to answer exam questions

APENDIX 5: Handling Documentary Evidence

Aims

The study skills learnt in this section should enable the student to: -

- Prepare effectively for exams

- Recognise the qualities needed to obtain a good exam pass

- Handle exam questions with quiet confidence

- Follow a definite timetable when answering exam questions

- Answer <u>only</u> the set questions

- Structure the exam answers

- Be aware of and avoid the causes of exam failure

Section 1: Opening Comments

After making necessary allowance for personal ability and other factors like personal health, acquiring effective exam skills is an absolute *'must'* for the student who wishes to do well. Their use enables the student to minimise the risk of failure and to gain the best possible marks.

Section 2: Qualities Required

To gain a good mark in an exam it's necessary to be: -

2.1   Efficient – keep to a timetable

2.2   Constantly focused – always bearing the question in mind

2.3   Organised – writing a **beginning, middle** and an **end**

2.4   Confident and sound in the subject knowledge – gained only by thorough revision

2.5   Pragmatic – tackling only those questions concerning which the student has some adequate knowledge

2.6   Able to prioritise – sifting relevant from irrelevant source material

Section 3: Common Reasons for Exam Failure

The most common reasons for exam failure are: -

3.1   A less than adequate grasp of the subject

3.2   Laziness or an inability to learn from previous mistakes

3.3   Not acknowledging both sides of an issue

3.4   The presentation of only one side of an argument

3.5   A weak or missing central theme

3.6   A lack of planning and preparation

3.7   A poor selection of the set questions

3.8   Rushing into a question without due care and attention

3.9   The over-use of emotive language or the giving of dogmatic assertions to mask a lack of knowledge, *e.g. "All Free Schools provoke educational inequality."*

3.10   Giving an irrelevant answer unrelated to the Title

3.11   *'Cramming in'* everything known about a topic in the hope of answering some aspects of the question

3.12   Giving unjustified conclusions, or conclusions which simply repeat the main body of the assignment

3.13   Over-confidence leading to careless mistakes

3.14   Under-confidence leading to a timid refusal to answer questions for fear of making a mistake

3.15   Barely using either primary or secondary research when both are needed to answer the question

3.16   Using poor quality, irrelevant, or *'too narrow a range'* of source material

3.17   Blatant plagiarism (presenting another person's answers as one's own)

3.18   Rushing into giving an answer with barely any consideration given to an Introduction, Conclusion or any basic structure

Section 4: More Reasons for Exam Failure

Other reasons for exam failure consist of: -

4.1   Answering another (hoped-for) question rather than the one being asked, by: -

4.1.1   Answering a question as if it were the one the student had hoped *'would come up'*

4.1.2   Answering a question that came up in the previous year's exam

4.1.3   Answering a question which had been previously discussed with the tutor or with other fellow students

4.2   Omitting vital pieces of information, due to: -

4.2.1   Exam time running out

4.2.2   A lack of subject knowledge

4.2.3   A lack of realism – if the examiner knows it already (which he should), so that it needn't be said at all!

4.3   Poor presentation, including the use of: -

4.3.1   Bad grammar, punctuation and spelling

4.3.2   Inadequate vocabulary or use of jargon

4.3.3 The use of clichés and colloquialisms (slang, sloppy expressions or phrases)

4.3.4   Irrelevant material

4.3.5   Scrappy and/or over-detailed diagrams and tables

4.3.6   Verbosity – using unnecessary or long words when shorter words or phrases would do

Section 5: Exam Preparation

In the days <u>before</u> any exam, it's important to: -

5.1 Acknowledge that, whilst a certain amount of bodily tension can be productive, should it reach the point where distressing physical symptoms occur (*i.e.* sleeplessness or vomiting) then <u>professional help must be sought.</u> It would be detrimental to exam success should the student simply suffer in silence

5.2 Employ the final days in <u>revising that work which has already been done,</u> rather than in attempting any other work which has been neglected

5.3 Ensure that thorough revision is balanced by plenty of sleep and outdoor exercise

5.4 Ensure stationery is in good working order with spare pens available

5.5 Arrive at the exam hall in plenty of time, giving generous allowance for delays

5.6 Use the toilet <u>ten</u> minutes before the exam begins. Drink only a few sips of water <u>twenty</u> minutes before the exam begins

5.7 Neatly arrange any stationery and resolve, during natural pauses throughout the exam, only to look up at the ceiling, or at the clock, but <u>not</u> at any other person

5.8 Understand the meaning of common exam words **(Appendix 1)**

5.9 Understand who the examiners are likely to be and what they are wanting. (In **'A'** level exams they rarely have more than ten minutes to spare for each essay before allocating a grade – see **Appendix 2**)

Section 6: Approaching Exam Questions

When approaching, an exam question it's necessary to: -

6.1   Avoid wishful thinking *i.e.* hoping that the question means something different from what it's saying

6.2   Decide <u>precisely</u> what the question is asking

6.3   See whether <u>all</u> parts of the question can be answered

6.4   Sift <u>carefully</u> through the wording and use *'question dissection'* to identify: -

6.4.1   The main subject

6.4.2   The precise instruction

6.4.3   Key words and phrases

6.4.4   The relevant time-scale

(See **Appendix 3** for further details)

6.5   Write an *'outline plan'* in either simple list form or in the form of a thought shower. Be careful not to use up too much time on this, **(Appendix 4).**

Section 7: Time Management

With a four-question essay, three-hour exam, it may prove useful to follow this timetable: -

Time

0.00   Turn the paper over

0.05   Read through the paper carefully. Begin *'question dissection'* **(Appendix 3)**

0.15   Tackle the first question – spend <u>5 minutes</u> writing an *'outline plan'*

0.50   Complete answering the first question (35 minutes long)

1.15   Plan the other three questions in a similar manner to the first

1.50   Write out the second answer in 35 minutes

2.25   Write out the third answer in 35 minutes

3.00   Write out the fourth answer in 35 minutes

In the event of any spare time, ensure that the question <u>numbers</u> are correct and match those of the exam paper. Insert any missing information into **Appendices** or **Footnotes** at the end of the essay. Correct any serious spelling and linguistic mistakes.

It may be best to begin answering the easiest question first, rather than following a strict numerical sequence. However, if this approach is followed then <u>extra care should be taken to</u>

ensure that the answer number corresponds to the question number. This would guard against unnecessary failure.

Follow the correct procedures for handling documentary evidence, **(Appendix 5).**

A degree of variation may be permitted when using the above timetable, *i.e.* two essay plans could be written out at the beginning, followed by another two around the middle of the exam. Doing this would serve as a mental *'break'* (as would a stretch of one's arms or legs.) What should be avoided is a protracted period spent writing out four long essay answers, one after the other. This would simply create exhaustion and a loss of marks; careless mistakes would result from poor concentration.

Section 8: Answering Exam Questions

When answering an Exam Paper, it's necessary to: -

8.1 Answer all the required Questions. Remember, it's easier to gain the first **50%** of marks rather than the second **50%** (see **Appendix 2**)

8.2 Answer the set question (not to do so guarantees failure)

8.3 Clearly define any terms used

8.4 Disagree politely when giving valid reasons against something

8.5 Enjoy the work as much as possible

8.6 Be honest: don't hide any ignorance behind: -

8.6.1 Apologetic pleading *i.e. 'I regret to say that ...'*

8.6.2 Empty superlatives *i.e. 'fantastic,' 'marvellous' or 'terrific'*

8.6.3 Excessive dogmatism *i.e. 'unfair' or 'unjust'*

8.6.4 Pomposity i.e. *"In my opinion, this highly speculative hypothesis tends to be rather unsound and not based upon valid primary and secondary data"*

8.7 Should an important point have been accidently omitted, resist the temptation to cram it into the *'main body'* of the essay; doing so would simply result in an untidy mess. The better option is to write out the point as a **Footnote** or (if it is a very long point) as an **Appendix.** Draw the examiner's attention to it by placing an asterisk (*) in the space where the point would originally have been made.

8.8 In exam questions *'Discuss'* means to argue points *'for'* and *'against.'*
'Outline' means to *'Briefly describe.'*

Section 9: Structuring Exam Answers

An exam answer is best structured as follows: -

9.1 **An Introduction** containing: -

9.1.1 A gripping opening sentence (or quotation)

9.1.2 An outline of the subject (with a brief explanation of its importance)

9.1.3 Key definitions and a thumbnail sketch of the main ideas

9.2 **A main body** consisting of: -

9.2.1 An ordered line of reasoning based upon a few core ideas

9.2.2 Supporting evidence *i.e.* examples and data

9.2.3 Diagrams and Tables; because this is an Exam Paper these can be inserted into the *'main body'* of the essay. They add to the general flow of the work.

9.3 **A Conclusion** containing: -

9.3.1 A summary of the main ideas

9.3.2 A firm or tentative answer, wholly related to the set Question and to the **main body** of the essay

9.3.3 A mention of wider implications, i.e. likely future trends and the possibility of further research

9.3.4 A concise closing comment or *'punch line,'* bringing the essay to a definite end

Section 10: Closing Comments

Perhaps the most tragic situation in Exams is not failure itself but failure when the student possessed the ability to obtain a good pass. It's precisely this kind of situation that examination techniques have been designed to prevent. **Their use is vital.** Finally, always remember to turn over the exam paper. It's amazing just how many (otherwise sensible students) can forget to observe this simple common-sense rule.

Appendix 1: A List of 'Instruction Words' Used in Exams

1.	Account for...	18.	How far...?
2.	Analyse...	19.	Illustrate...
3.	Assess...	20.	Interpret...
4.	Comment...	21.	Justify...
5.	Compare and contrast...	22.	List...
6.	Consider...	23.	Outline...
7.	Criticise...	24.	Prove...
8.	Define...	25.	Read...
9.	Demonstrate...	26.	Reconcile...
10.	Describe...	27.	Relate...
11.	Discuss...	28.	Review...
12.	Distinguish...	29.	Show how...
13.	Enumerate...	30.	State...
14.	Evaluate...	31.	Study...
15.	Examine...	32.	Summarise...
16.	Explain...	33.	To what extent...?
17.	Give reasons for...	34.	Trace...

The meaning of each of these words can be found in any good dictionary

Appendix 2: 'A' Level Grades

Grade %

A*:	**80** Excellent Pass
A:	**70** Very Good Pass
B:	**60-69** Good Pass
C:	**53-59** Pass
D:	**46-52** Pass
E:	**40-45** Narrow Pass
N:	**35-39** Narrow Fail
U:	**Not** Graded Fail

Marks in the **40%** area are regarded as a *'borderline pass'* or *'fail'* and may have to be re-marked to assess their final grade.

Appendix 3: 'Question Dissection'

When approaching an exam question like, *"What were the causes of the French Revolution in 1789? Was its descent into violence inevitable?"* it's <u>vitally important</u> to read (and re-read) the *'set Question'* carefully before: -

1) Dividing the question into digestible chunks using /

2) Boxing *'instructing'* words like *'what,' 'why,'* *'Discuss'* or *'critically analyse'*   [   ]

3) <u>Underlining</u> key words

4) Placing key dates, locations, words or phrases in boxed brackets [ ]

5) Circling any plurals   ◯

When this happens, the original question assumes the form that's written out below: -
|What| were the caus(es)of /the [French] <u>Revolution</u> <u>[in 1789]</u>? |Was| its <u>descent</u> /into <u>violence</u> inevitable?

In this case, *'question dissection'* has provided cues to help the student to remember to answer <u>both</u> parts of the question.

However, it's important to use either a pencil or different coloured pen when dissecting a question otherwise it could look as its being crossed out in a very messy fashion. When this happens, important wording could be obscured and marks lost thus.

Appendix 4: Planning to Answer Exam Questions

Sketch a *'rough and ready'* plan of the order in which the answer should be written: -
1)   <u>Underline</u> those parts that must be given priority

2)   Place a question mark (?) against those parts which <u>may</u> possibly be included

3)   Cross out ~~irrelevant~~ parts

When writing out the answer it's vital to: -

1)   Reword the question in the introduction

2)   <u>Check halfway</u> through the essay to see if the *'set Question'* is still being answered

3)   <u>Check again towards the end</u> that the *set Question'* has been answered as fully as possible

Appendix 5: Handling Documentary Evidence

During exam revision Documentary Research requires three methods of investigation: -

- Basic literary sources: these provide knowledge about the subject and establishment of a chronology.
- Other, more sophisticated sources *e.g.* scientific text books or magazines *e.g.* The Lancet Medical Journal
- Specialised sources – *e.g.* television, radio documentaries and electronic sources

The Snowball Effect

This occurs when one source of information leads to another – rather like an expanding snowball. A start is made with <u>B</u>asic Sources like a text book **(B)** before moving onto more <u>S</u>pecialised Sources like a journal article **(S)** and finally to <u>T</u>ertiary **(T)** or miscellaneous other sources which may only be of interest to the researcher. This progress from one type of source to another is illustrated in the diagram below.

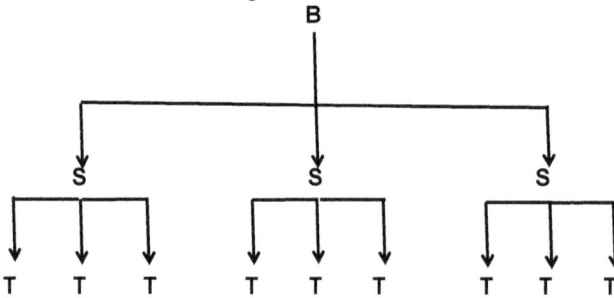

The Five '*W's*' Levels of explanation

For further details, please refer to the comments on the bottom of **p.137**

PART 2: REVISION AIDS

(Mainly for those studying in the Humanities, Business Studies and Social sciences)

REVISION AIDS 1:
FOUNDATION LEVEL

Contents

1) DAEJ

2) DEARS

3) DEEPS

4) GCSE Business Studies Project Checklist

5) How best to analyse poetry

6) How best to criticise poetry

7) How best to handle historical sources

8) How best to interpret statistics

9) What is History?

10) What makes a great life?

DAEJ

DAEJ – facilitates the planning and writing of *'Advanced'* and *'Degree Level'* exam essays by ensuring that <u>D</u>escription, <u>A</u>nalysis, <u>E</u>valuation and <u>J</u>ustification are given full attention: -

'Description' – outlines what a thing (or theory) consists of and provides vital background information to the set *'Exam Question.'*

'Analysis' – explains <u>why</u> a thing (or theory) exists (or why an event happened). It may begin with a simple assessment of the *'positives'* and *'negatives'* before turning to more complex forms of questioning and interpretation. Both quantitative and qualitative evidence must be used to support or refute any analysis.

'Evaluation' – decides whether a thing (or a theory) is valid (accurate, true and relevant), partly valid, or invalid. It is a reasoned conclusion that directly answers the question set by the examiner. It may also point out the likely consequences of a recommended course of action.

'Justification' – gives the reasons why a certain evaluation has been put forward. It briefly refers to previously-mentioned evidence to defend the conclusion. A good justification prevents any evaluation from becoming a mere dogmatic assertion.

<u>**N.B:**</u> At *'A'* level, the student must learn to move from **D,** to **J** to get good marks. To stop at **D** results in failure; to stop at **A** scrapes only a bare pass or even failure again. *'E'* and *'J'* <u>must be included</u> to achieve a good grade.

DEARS

'Dears' stands for **D**iagram, **E**xplanation, **A**ssociation, **R**ecall and **S**ummary and is an <u>easy</u> way to learn textbook (or one's own) **Diagrams** and **Tables.**

'Diagram' – the actual textbook (or a personally created) Diagram or Statistical Table

'Explanation' – gives the meaning of a Diagram or Statistical Table

'Association' – links a Diagram to key related ideas and phraseology, *e.g.* a diagram illustrating the operation of *'demand and supply'* (found online or in any Economics textbook) which is associated with the key idea of *'scarcity'*

'Recall' – memorises all the above details with the aid of memory techniques (outlined in *'Section 3'* of *'Study Aid 2'*)

'Summary' – makes a concise list of ALL the details (taken from the Diagram or Table) in either written (or verbal) form

Should time permit, it may be helpful when drawing up a Diagram to follow a *'Crimean'* colour scheme: -

Black: for axes and Main Title

Blue: for wording

Red: for figures

Green: for names

Grey: for shading and the highlighting of key points

Lines on a graph or bars on a chart may be in any of the above colours. However, in order not to annoy or puzzle readers <u>all</u> Diagrams must be accompanied by a relevant explanation.

DEEPS

'DEEPS' stands for the **D**escription, **E**xplanation, **E**valuation, **P**rescription and **S**ummary of financial information: -

DESCRIPTION: *"What do the figures reveal about an Organization's health?"*

EXPLANATION: *"Why do the figures reveal it?"*

EVALUATION: *"Is the explanation for these figures plausible?"*

PRESCRIPTION: *"What should be done in response to these figures?"*

SUMMARY: *"What conclusion(s) can be drawn from these figures?"*

'DEEPS' provides an excellent framework when answering questions on Business Finance. It deals with any sudden mental block by constantly moving thought processes along toward a conclusion (Summary).

In relation to *'low mark'* questions a stop can be made with **D**escription. However, *'higher mark'* questions (involving accounts interpretation) require the whole of *'DEEPS.'* In addition, the final **S**ummary <u>must</u> give a reasoned answer and relate directly to the Exam Question.

'DEEPS' can also help in the planning and compiling of Financial Reports.

GCSE BUSINESS STUDIES PROJECT CHECKLIST

Have the exam criteria and syllabus requirements all been met?

HAVE YOU: -	SCORE
1) Listed clear aims?	0 1 2 3
2) Selected the industry you want to be in?	0 1 2 3
3) Decided upon the type of Business Organisation?	0 1 2 3
4) Chosen your Retail Outlet?	0 1 2 3
5) Decided upon the location of your Outlet?	0 1 2 3
6) Visited and checked sited and mapped your location?	0 1 2 3
7) Accurately the accessibility of your location?	0 1 2 3
8) Obtained planning permission?	0 1 2 3
9) Completed any background reading and secondary research?	0 1 2 3
10) Surveyed retailers to assess the level of demand?	0 1 2 3
11) Conducted a consumer survey?	0 1 2 3
12) Reviewed the results of your Market Research?	0 1 2 3
13) Estimated *'setting-up'* costs?	0 1 2 3
14) Completed a *'break-even'* analysis?	0 1 2 3
15) Completed a *'Cash Flow'* forecast?	0 1 2 3
16) Considered alternative sources of finance?	0 1 2 3
17) Visited a Bank to obtain financial information?	0 1 2 3
18) Decided upon the methods to use regarding advertising and publicity?	0 1 2 3
19) Considered how to recruit, train and hold staff?	0 1 2 3
20) Assessed staffing costs and numbers required?	0 1 2 3
21) Given a <u>realistic</u> forecast of future developments?	0 1 2 3
22) Cited previously gathered evidence in one's conclusions?	0 1 2 3
23) Employed a variety of graphical presentations?	0 1 2 3
24) Checked that the information given makes sense?	0 1 2 3
25) Checked that all listed aims have been met?	0 1 2 3

Key
0 = Task not completed
1 = Minor completion of task
2 = Some completion of task
3 = Task completed

HOW BEST TO ANALYSE POETRY?

An effective way to interpret a poem is to read through it carefully (at least two or three times) before asking the following questions: -

1) What first impressions did the poem make?
2) Was the poem easy or difficult to understand?
3) When was, the poem written?
4) What was the poem's context (or setting)?
5) Where was, it written?
6) Who wrote it and were they famous either during or after their lifetime?
7) What political or other constraints existed when it was written?
8) Why was it written?
9) What was the poet's personal background?
10) Was the poet pursuing a secret agenda?
11) Who was the original intended audience?
12) Was the audience homogeneous (consisting of the same type of people) or mixed?
13) Was the poem comical, didactic, metaphysical, pastoral, satirical or tragic?
14) Was the poem action, character or idea-centred?
15) Did the poem tell a story (narrative)?
16) Was the narrative linear (with a beginning, middle or end) or circular (going back and forth with the aid of flashbacks)?
17) Did the poem convey a message?
18) What was the poem's basic philosophy (or belief system)?
19) How coherent was its philosophy?
20) Who could benefit or be harmed by this philosophy?
21) Was the poem markedly biased in favour of or against something?
22) How strong was its bias?
23) Did it adopt a first or third person viewpoint?
24) What tone was adopted?
25) Did the tone change and if so why?
26) Was it in *'fixed'* or *'free'* verse form?
27) How many verses were there?
28) Were the verses regular or irregular in their size?
29) Were the verses rhyming or non-rhyming?
30) Was there a rhythmic beat to the poem?
31) Was the style ornate, formal, informal or colloquial?
32) What was the prevailing mood (or emotion) in the poem?
33) Did the prevailing mood change and why?
34) Were visual representations (*e.g.* photographs) used in the poem?
35) Were stylistic devices employed *e.g.* alliterations or assonances?
36) Were metaphors and similes used to create imagery?
37) Were specific linguistic devices used *e.g.* onomatopoeia?
38) Was a *'persona'* adopted?
39) Was *'animation'* used?
40) What embedded facts, (if any) lay hidden within the poem?
41) Was the poem pure fantasy?
42) What did the poem mean?
43) Did it contain both explicit and implicit meanings?
44) Were there any alternative interpretations?
45) Why were alternative interpretations accepted (or rejected) by the reader?
46) What would the original audience have felt about the poem?
47) How did the poem make me feel and why?

48) Could the poem be summarised in a couple of sentences?

49) Did the poem achieve what it set out to do?

50) Could the poet have done better and if so, how?

51) What lessons could be learnt from the poem?

52) Would I like to read the poem again?

53) Did I manage to enter the mind of the poet and feel what he or she felt – even though it may have been depressing?

54) What score out of ten would I give the poem, and why?

Use relevant quotations and supporting evidence to add further clarity to any given answer. The examiner would expect the reader to fully engage with and respond to the poem on a personal as well as an intellectual level. However, not all the above questions need to be asked concerning every poem. The meaning of descriptive terms like *'pastoral'* or *'satirical'* can be found in any standard dictionary or textbook on poetry. The same point also applies to more specialised terms like *'alliteration'* or *'assonance.'* It's often helpful to consult with one's teacher or a bookshop salesperson to purchase a dictionary which suits ones needs.

HOW BEST TO CRITICISE POETRY?

The following statements should enable a poet to increase his/her capacity to receive constructive criticism in relation to their own poetry. **Question 1** asks whether the poem has demonstrated certain strengths and **question 2** whether it has avoided (and sometimes common) weaknesses.

1) This poem needs to have demonstrated: -
1.1 Why it was written
1.2 For whom it was written
1.3 Where and when was it set
1.4 Whether it adopted a didactic or hedonistic approach
1.5 Whether it followed a universal or theme
1.6 A stirring appropriate emotions
1.7 A conveyance of an intended mood
1.8 A provocation of an emotive response (either a *'wow'* or *'I've learned something useful'* reaction)
1.9 An entertainment and/or educational function
1.10 A clear (either circular, linear or narrative) structure
1.11 A consistent viewpoint
1.12 A sufficient vocabulary
1.13 An appropriate use of formal or informal language
1.14 A style that fits the subject matter
1.15 A skilful use of imagery
1.16 A talent for using literary devices *e.g.* personification and rhetorical questions
1.17 An ability to display interesting ideas
1.18 A wise sensitivity to its subject matter
1.19 Either a topical and/or historical awareness
1.20 Courage in tackling controversial issues
1.21 A tendency to provoke discussion and thought
1.22 An appropriate use of humour
1.23 A vivid characterisation of people, place and setting
1.24 Evidence of learning from previous poetical traditions
1.25 An attractive, eye-catching format
1.26 Some originality
1.27 An appropriate length
1.28 Evidence of careful editing
1.29 A capacity to leave the reader wanting more
1.30 A strong, rather than a vague, or meandering close

2) This poem needs to have avoided the following weaknesses: -
2.1 A failure to display (the above listed) strengths
2.2 Lack of clarity
2.3 Irritating self-pity
2.4 The use of too many clichés
2.5 Inappropriate language
2.6 Unoriginal imagery and phraseology
2.7 Redundant phrases and adjectives
2.8 Superficial comments
2.9 Gross insensitivity
2.10 Trite superficiality
2.11 Unnecessary repetition
2.12 Trying to explain things as one went along

2.13 Inappropriate line breaks
2.14 Boring, annoying or baffling phraseology
2.15 A rambling, tedious length
2.16 A failure to leave enough to the imagination
2.17 Serious factual mistakes
2.18 Pretentious pomposity
2.19 A hectoring style, which arrogantly tells the reader what they should or should not think
2.20 The use of outdated satire
2.21 The incitement of religious, racial or political hatred
2.22 A weak ending

In addition, <u>it's vitally important to be able to accept as well as give criticism.</u> Any failure to do this means that one won't be able to develop as a poet. Sometimes, it's necessary to accept that much time has been spent producing a poem that doesn't work. In such cases, it's best to leave the poem to one side and come back to it with a fresh mind before taking a final decision to either improve or abandon it.

HOW BEST TO HANDLE HISTORICAL SOURCES?

When confronted by a historical source take the following steps.

Step 1: Read through the Source (and any questions asked about it) two or three times, highlighting key points.

Step 2: Briefly list the strengths and weaknesses of the historical source

Step 3: Use a tally score of **0** to **5** (see key at bottom of page) to assess it's: -
- **Validity** – is it truthful and relevant?
- **Reliability** – can it be confirmed by other reputable sources?
- **Integrity** – how honest is the author?
- **Typicality** – how representative is it?

Step 4: Record any original thoughts or criticisms and decide whether to use them in any final evaluation

Step 5: List any points concerning the Source (or words that are difficult to understand) and draft a brief provisional answer to each one

Step 6: Begin a detailed to answer any questions about the Source

Step 7: Keep referring to the Source when answering any questions

Key

0 = Not valid (reliable, honest or typical)
1 = Very weakly valid (reliable, honest or typical)
2 = Weakly valid (reliable, honest or typical)
3 = Moderately valid (reliable, honest or typical)
4 = Strongly valid (reliable, honest or typical)
5 = Very strongly valid (reliable, honest or typical)

In explaining historical sources the *'When?' 'Where?' 'Who?'* and *'What?'* must be answered before the *'Why?'* Remember, trying to explain the *'Why'* without having the other *'Ws'* in place gives a bad *'W,'* which is *'Waffle'* (long winded nonsense). To obtain high marks it's important to ascend the appropriate levels of explanation – whilst always being careful to answer the question that's been set, (See the diagram in **Study Aid 12, Appendix 5, p.124)**

HOW BEST TO INTERPRET STATISTICS?

When confronted by statistics in a data response question stay calm! Breathe in and out slowly and deeply, counting to five; then study each question carefully Practise *'Question Dissection'* **(p.123)** and do the following: -

1. Read the **Title** (and **sub-titles**) above a Statistical Table (or Graph) to discover <u>exactly</u> what is being measured.

2. Look down the **vertical** and across the **horizontal** axes to see what is being measured against what.

3. Study the figures to see whether they cover a moment in time or apply only to **a set period**. If the latter applies, look for the following types of trend: -
3.1 Upward
3.2 Downward
3.3 Flat (also known as **plateau** or **stable**)
3.4 Cyclical (also known as **seasonal** if the cycle occurs within one year)
3.5 Random
3.6 Combined *e.g.* an upward cyclical trend

4. Take *great* care to: -
4.1 *Always turn over* the examination question paper
4.2 Answer *only* the set question
4.3 Answer *all* parts of the question
4.4 Quote *relevant* facts and figures
4.5 Use *appropriate* business or sociological words
4.6 *Write* tidy and regularly spaced paragraphs

However, the best way to handle statistics is regular practice through using calculators and relevant computerised packages. Like other forms of numeric work the best form of learning is *'learning by doing.'*

WHAT IS HISTORY?

History – is the collective memory of humanity, telling the story of the past. It's the organised investigation and study of past events and long-term changes. Generally, history involves looking at the *'5W's'* of: -

- Who?
- What?
- When?
- Where?
- Why?

This means that history can be divided into the following five categories: -

1) Narrative History – recounting the story of past events – <u>what</u> happened, <u>where</u> it happened, <u>when</u> it happened and to <u>whom</u>

2) Analytical History – explaining the past by looking at <u>why</u> things happened

3) Moralistic History – evaluating the past in the form of value judgements. Was a past event a good or a bad thing and can any lessons be learnt from it?

4) Philosophical History – uncovering the recurrent themes and patterns of behaviour seen throughout historical events; deciding whether history is tending toward a direction.

5) Applied History – looking at <u>how</u> the lessons learnt from the past can help us in the present.

Historical Interpretation – explaining, interpreting and drawing conclusions about the past from the available evidence

Family History – the history of a family or related group of families

Local History – the history of an area or locality

Not only can history be a story, a record of facts and an investigation into the past, but it also often involves a systematic study of change.

Change – an alteration in any form of state; a movement from one condition toward another over a period (which may cause a loss in the original nature of the object undergoing the change). There are five types of change, each one distinct from the other: -

1) Dialectic(al) Change – any change resulting from a compromise between two (reconcilable) opposites, which then merge together to form a synthesis, *e.g.* the *'midi'* skirt being a compromise between the *'mini'* and *'maxi'* skirt.

2) Dichotomous Change – any change resulting from a clash of irreconcilable opposites, where one opposite must give way in total defeat to the other. There can be no compromise between the opposing factors, e.g. the war between Hitler and Stalin.

3) Historical Change – how one form of society (or group of societies) changes into another, spanning different historical periods *e.g.* the movement from Feudalism to Capitalism in Europe from 1350-1850; a study of this type of change is useful in offering a very long-term perspective.

4) Overarching Change – powerful, revolutionary change which arises from (and then proceeds to affect) most areas of a society, *i.e.* The Industrial Revolution. A study of this type of change is useful when assessing its impact across the whole of a given society.

5) Societal Change – changes in the behaviour, social relationships and structures of a given society (or group of societies) during one historical period. A change to the status of the peasantry in Medieval England is one example. Studying this type of change is useful when offering a short, middle or long-term perspective.

Change can impact upon whole communities of people.

Community – a clearly defined social unit containing a distinct pattern of human relationships. Interaction within a community helps to mould a person's individual identity. Communities can be viewed in geographical or non-geographical terms *i.e.* the East End Community of London or the global *'Community'* of Financiers.

The word *'Community'* really has taken on many meanings, *i.e.*
- A specific locality or neighbourhood *i.e.* the Village Community
- A general cluster of diverse social relationships *i.e.* the Internet Community
- A kind of relationship *i.e.* the International Financial Community
The first example represents a geographical locatable community; whilst the second two are not specifically geographical but are spread over an indefinite area.

Community can also influence the formation of individual identity.

Identity – the collection of core personality traits, attitudes, beliefs and abilities, which form the very essence of a person. An *'identity'* distinguishes one person from another.

WHAT MAKES A GREAT LIFE?

ome are born to greatness, some achieve greatness and others have it thrust upon
em" (William Shakespeare, Twelfth Night 1602*)*

GREAT LIFE – a life having a major and lasting impact upon human affairs'; either
nstructive or destructive in its outworking – a *'Great Life'* does not necessarily mean a
orally *'good life.'*

REATNESS – having exceptional personal qualities and abilities which give a person
owering stature over his/her fellow human beings

OSTHUMOUS RECOGNITION – the type of recognition and fame which comes
ly after death

hen studying a *'Great Life'* it's helpful to ask the following questions: -

How do we know about a Great Life?

o discover more about a *'Great Life'* we need to look to: -

rimary Sources – derived from letters, accounts, diaries, business documents

econdary Sources – family tradition, studies by historians, psychological analyses

rtefacts – clothes, personal effects, gravestone inscriptions, physical remains

cientific Research – DNA analysis, carbon dating of primitive organic material, *e.g.*
ones, which help date the approximate period in which a person lived

How can we find out the truth about a Great Life?

'Great Life,' by its very definition, tends to produce many sources of valuable
formation. A lack of knowledge is simply not a problem – rather *'information*
verload' constitutes something of a challenge. Some self-proclaimed individuals like
ulius Caesar or **Queen Elizabeth I** went to great lengths to produce their own
ffective self-publicity (and were often very *'economical with the truth.'*) Learning
ore of any *'Great Life'* needs an in-depth understanding of the customary ways of
inking during the historical period in which that life was lived.

ome of the truth about a *'Great Life'* can be found by carefully sifting through the
vidence and by addressing such questions as *'How did X feel when Y happened?'* or
'How was X affected by his/her childhood?' A journalistic approach is needed – with as
any relevant information sources as can be found – so building up a coherent picture
f the life under scrutiny. A great deal of mental application and collaborative research
ith other parties is needed to study a *'Great Life.'*

Sometimes *'greatness'* may take some considerable time to be appreciated, *i.e.* **Karl Marx** lived in obscurity throughout his lifetime and became famous only after his death; his was a **posthumous recognition.** Conversely, those who are famous now may well become forgotten within a generation. Moreover, a *'Great Life'* tends to be surrounded by many myths and controversies which tend to obscure the truth. Discovering more about a *'Great Life'* is a thoroughly fascinating exercise but it can be very time-consuming and demanding as historical research is rarely straightforward or easy. However, there's the joy of making new discoveries and learning some very profound moral lessons.

3) How Are Great Lives Made?

Understanding how a *'Great Life'* is made requires the use of *'OATS'* Analysis. This shows how *'greatness'* may come about through: -

Opportunity for advancement and the gaining of leadership skills
Ability and motivation
Timing and location

*'**S**pin'* *i.e.* the publicity that artificially inflates a person's reputation (for good or ill – depending upon the circumstances)

∴ OATS ⇒ Greatness

An absence of at least one of these three components prevents a life from ever becoming *'great'* (in the sense of having a major impact upon human affairs).

Conclusion:

The study of a *'Great Life'* is intriguing, bringing us into contact with a hugely complex (but always interesting) individual. It requires us to understand the relationship between such concepts as *'fame'* and *'success.'* When finding out about a *'Great Life'* our challenge is to: -

Study – what happened in this person's life
Examine – why this person became *'great?'*
Evaluate –the outcome of their life – was it good or bad?
Learn – the lessons to be gained from this person's life?

∴ SEEL ⇒ knowledge, understanding and evaluation of a great life

REVISION AIDS 2: INTERMEDIATE LEVEL

Contents

1) CESSPITTS Analysis

2) Contents of a Business Plan

3) How best to handle Business Case Studies

4) How to learn formulae without panicking

5) Key phrases for sociology essays

6) Sociological Perspectives

7) The difference between a *'sound'* and an *'unsound'* theory

8) The stages of Questionnaire design

9) The *'Syllabus Summary method'*

CESSPITTS ANALYSIS

CESSPITTS is an analytical tool, used to scrutinise the cultural, economic, social, structural, political, individual, technological, traditional and strategic causes and/or consequences of any major change within human society.

Cultural causes/consequences:
The values, norms, informal rules and way of life within a society as expressed in its art, music, philosophy literature, manufactured products and written laws

Economic causes/consequences:
The availability, production, distribution and consumption of goods and services, often expressed in the laws of *'supply and demand'*

Social causes/consequences:
The human interaction, peer pressure, the influence of leaders and the type of relationships existing within a group

Structural causes/consequences:
The structures and hierarchies within large government or non-government organizations and institutions

Political causes/consequences:
The distribution of power and factional conflicts within an institution, organization or small group setting

Individual causes/consequences:
The personal psychology, including attitude, belief, intellectual ability, emotional disposition, behavioural proclivity and volitional capacity (ability to make choices)

Technological causes/consequences:
The scientific and technological developments – one example being the rise of Information and Communication Technology (ICT)

Traditional causes/consequences:
The long-held custom, historical experience and the influence of religion; each passed down through succeeding generations

Strategic causes/consequences:
The geography, climate, terrain, natural resources and location of an area

CESSPITTS provides a logical *'step-by-step'* analysis of all the elements underlying changes within any human society the world over. However, there's no mention of *'language'* throughout **CESSPITTS** as it's not seen as being a barrier to fundamental changes taking place within society. Indeed, language often just reflects the changes happening in the areas listed by **CESSPITTS.**

CONTENTS OF A BUSINESS PLAN

Title Page

Contents Page

Executive Summary (Consisting of one point per chapter)

1. Service description, location and aims of the business

2. Project history and status

3. Situational Analysis (**S**trengths, **W**eaknesses, **O**pportunities & **T**hreats)

4. Markets, Marketing, Selling, Promotion and Pricing (either *'online'* or *'offline'*)

5. Technology & Production Considerations
- Purchasing plans
- Inventory system
- Space required
- Equipment required

6. Organization and Staffing (The advantages of being a *'Freelancer'* or a *'Sole Trader'*)

7. Legal, Contractual, Ethical & Copyright Considerations

8. Sources of Funding
- Financing Strategy
  - Alternative Sources of Funding
  - Application for Funds

9. Financial Plan: Budget and Forecast
- Revenue Projections, (*'Break Even'* Analysis)
- *'Start-Up'* Costs
- Cash Flow Projections
- Pro-Forma Statements
  - Balance Sheet
  - Income and Expenses, (Trading, Profit & Loss Account)
- Financial Ratios
- Preferred Banking Arrangements
- Cash and Credit Policies
- Methods of Credit Control

10. Taxation, Pensions and National Insurance (Check VAT rate)

11. Level of Risk: Insurance, Liability and *'Back-Up'* plans

12. Conclusion (main justification for investing in the Business)

Appendices (Containing Tables, Graphs & Documents)

- Visual Exhibits
- Results of Market Research
- Letterheads and Documentation
- Price lists
- List of Leasehold improvements
- List of existing Inventories
- Copies of Legal Agreements
- Letters of intent
- Details of Fund Providers
- List of Fixed Assets
- *'Break Even'* Chart
- Estimated Cash Flow for the first year
- Balance Sheet
- Estimated *'Trading Profit and Loss Account'*
- Sample Insurance Documents

References

- Name of present *'Lending Institution'*
- Lawyer's name (with contact details)
- Accountant's name (with contact details)
- Business Associates
- Information Sources (Authors and Acknowledgements)

HOW BEST TO HANDLE BUSINESS CASE STUDIES?

The following questions have been designed to encourage students to engage with Business Case Studies: -

1. Is the Case Study the <u>only</u> source of information or can more be gained from other sources?

2. Is it to be written as a Report or an Essay?

3. Have appropriate analytical tools been selected? Examples being: -
- **A SWOT Analysis** (to monitor the internal <u>s</u>trengths, and <u>w</u>eaknesses plus external <u>o</u>pportunities and <u>t</u>hreats facing a firm) and/or
- **A PESTEL Analysis** (the <u>p</u>olitical, <u>e</u>conomic, <u>s</u>ocial, <u>t</u>echnological, <u>e</u>nvironmental or <u>l</u>egal opportunities and threats facing a firm in its external environment)?

4. Have <u>relevant</u> theories been selected? What parts of the theory have been used? (Do <u>not</u> regurgitate everything known about a theory, unless clearly asked to do so.)

5. Does the Case Study require that you assume a distinct role, *i.e.* that of a Company Employee?

6. Has *'quantitative'* and *'qualitative'* information been considered? When interpreting any *'quantitative'* evidence, remember: -
- Stay calm
- Look at the figures
- Begin by looking at the Title and any Subtitles
- Look down and across the axes to see what measurements are being used
- Go into the details of the figures, looking for any upward, downward, stable, cyclic or mixed trends
- Suggest reasons <u>why</u> the figures follow a certain pattern, bearing in mind other explanations
- Show why one interpretation of the evidence should be given precedence over any others

7. Has notice been taken of things beginning to go wrong in an Organization, *e.g.* unmet orders?

8. Have there been <u>underlying</u> as well as <u>obvious</u> causes of problems, *("the cause of the causes?")*

9. Has the root problem of an Organization been located (and defined), *e.g.* an unwillingness to respond to change.

10. Does the Organization (or those responsible for it) have clear aims? If so, are these aims realistic and appropriate to the Business?

11. How well is the Organization coping with any changes in its environment?

12. Does the Company need to: -
- Totally change direction (either rapidly or slowly)?
- Simply improve upon what it's already doing?
- Does nothing but await future developments?

13. What resources are needed to help the Organization achieve its aims? Estimate the scale of those resources and suggest where they may be found. (These may include human as well as financial resources.)

14. Is the Case Study concise? Don't meander – keep to the points.

15. Are recommendations provided which: -
- Consider the resource constraints?
- Seek to resolve (or at least reduce) problems?
- Are realistic and achievable?
- Are comprehensive, addressing all areas of company activity *e.g.* production, promotion, price and place?
- Are measurable – with their effectiveness being open to quantitative assessment
- Are based upon available evidence?
- Form part of a coherent business strategy?
- Consider their possible effect upon workforce morale and management/employee relationships?

16. Are reasons given showing why particular recommendations have been made?

17. Why may one course of action have been followed over another?

18. Which of the following growth strategies (if any) has been followed?
- Greater market penetration
- Existing product in new markets.
- New product in existing markets.
- New product in new markets (*i.e.* diversification)

Are reasons given for following one or more of the above strategies? (Remember that the degree of risk increases the further down the list you go).

19. Where will the Company most likely be located *'geographically'* in the future?

20. Have figures been quoted to support relevant points?

21. Have Diagrams and Organizational Charts have been used to support the study? (They must never be overused and need always to be accompanied by an explanation).

Small Case Studies normally follow the order of the set question, whereas larger ones tend to observe the following structure:
- Introduction
- Analysis of the problem
- Suggested strategy
- Recommendations
- Justifications – showing how specific recommendations could benefit the Company
- Clear conclusions
- An Appendix (or Additional Information)
- A Bibliography

The last two points are unlikely to be required in exams.

HOW TO LEARN FORMULAE WITHOUT PANICKING

Many students are daunted by the learning and practise of formulae. However, the first thing to do when tackling them is to mentally stand back and take a deep breath. Calmly look at the formula and begin to deal with it in a step-by-step manner. Use the *'Crimean Colour Scheme'* (named after the colour of the army uniforms used in the Crimean War of 1854-1856) as demonstrated in the following formula: -

FORMULA ONE (F1) Quick ratio = Current assets - stock
                                                            Current liabilities

FORMULA TWO (F2)

Return on capital employed = Net Profit before tax + interest on loans x 100%
                                              Fixed Assets + (Current assets - Current liabilities)

Using *'the Crimean Colour Scheme'* it's necessary to: -

1. Write the formula in full whilst adopting a colour scheme in which: -
- The main variable (ratio) is written in **blue**
- Any underlining and mathematical symbols *i.e.* equal (=) and percentage (**%**) signs are written in **black**.
- The top half is written in red
- The bottom half is written in **green**
- Any key points are (with the aid of a pencil) shaded in *'grey.'*

For **FORMULA ONE (F1)** such a scheme would produce the following layout:

F1: - Quick ratio (BLUE) = (BLACK) Current Assets (RED) - Stock (RED)
                                                  Current liabilities (GREEN)

2. Whilst retaining the *'Crimean Colour Scheme,'* carefully: -
- Abbreviate the main variable to its capitalised initials (to **QR** in the case of *'F1'*).
- Denote the variables in the top line by the symbol *'a'* – but should more than one variable be present then use numbered **a's**, *e.g.* **a1, a2, a3...**
- Denote the variables in the bottom line by the symbol *'b'* – but should more than one variable be present then use numbered **b's**, *e.g.* **b1, b2, b3...**
- Denote any further variables by the symbol *'c'* – but should more than one variable be present then use numbered **c's**, *e.g.* **c1, c2, c3...**

By this *stage "Formula One"* should resemble: -

F1: QR = a1 - a2
                  b

3. Whilst retaining the above colour scheme, carefully: -
- Insert a *'key'* showing the meaning of each symbol. Thus, the link word *"Where"* should always introduce the key: -

Where: -
QR = Quick ratio
a1 = Current Assets
a2 = Stock
b = Current liabilities

- Use <u>repeated</u> recitation (aloud to yourself) to assimilate both the formula and the meaning of key symbols.
- Test your knowledge by <u>repeatedly</u> writing the above formula and key without referring to any books or notes.
- <u>Repeatedly</u> practise using the formula by employing real figures taken from textbooks or old exam papers.

The above method is clearly seen in the following example.

FORMULA TWO (F2)

Return on capital employed = <u>Net profit before tax + interest on loans</u> x 100%
                              Fixed assets + (Current assets – Current Liabilities)

F2: ROCE (BLUE) = (BLACK) <u>a1 + a2 (RED)</u> % (BLACK)
                        b1 + (b2 - b3) (GREEN)

Where: -
ROCE = Return on capital employed
a1 = Net profit before tax
a2 = Interest on loans
b1 = Fixed assets
b2 = Current assets
b3 = Current liabilities
% = x 100%

Breaking everything down into easily memorable symbols should (with practice) enable the student to understand, learn and apply those formulae that are relevant to their discipline. It also allows for the fact that mathematics is a logical subject which needn't be too daunting when the correct method of learning is adopted. This type of methodology contains some degree of flexibility; the above two formulae could retain capitalised initials (as seen in the examples on the next page).

A learning method of great assistance to one student may not be useful at all to another. People have different learning styles and it really is up to the student to decide which one feels best for them.

FORMULA ONE (F1)

Quick ratio = <u>Current Assets - Stock</u>
                  Current liabilities

F1: $QR = \dfrac{CA - S}{CL}$

Where: -
QR = Quick ratio
CA = Current Assets
S = Stock
CL = Current liabilities

FORMULA TWO (F2)

Return on capital employed = <u>Net profit before tax + interest on loans</u> x 100%
                                     Fixed assets + (Current assets - Current liabilities)

$$F2: ROCE = \dfrac{NP + I}{FA + (CA - CL)}\%$$

Where: -
ROCE = Return on capital employed
NP= Net profit before tax
I = Interest on loans
FA = Fixed assets
CA = Current assets
CL = Current liabilities
x 100% = convert into percentages
.

KEY PHRASES FOR SOCIOLOGY ESSAYS

Phrases to use in Introductions

'A popular (longstanding) debate in Sociology concerns...'

'The main issue under examination...'

'To answer (address) the question over whether...'

'This essay will argue...'

'The main argument of this essay is that...'

Phrases to use in the *'Main Body'*

'X claims (argues, asserts, states) that his viewpoint (hypothesis, suggestion) is correct. However, this is hotly (heavily) disputed (challenged, criticised) by a range of commentators (researchers, sociologists, social investigators) including X and Y. They instead suggest...

'One reason why X's findings (ideas, research, or a theory) have been challenged (disputed) is because...

'One (A) major strength (weakness, difficulty) in X's argument (research methodology) is (was)...

'The validity (reliability) of these findings (conclusions) can be challenged (criticised) because (for the following reasons that...)'

'Sociologists like X and Y have long been divided (in dispute) over the issue of...'

'It is (was) suggested (postulated) by X that...'

'An alternative suggestion made (put forward by) ...'

'X claimed to have evidence to support the argument (hypothesis, view) that... but his evidence (findings, research) is doubtful (debatable, disputed, questionable, questioned) because (on the grounds that) ...

'Sociologists would (not) support the argument (opinion, stance, view) of X as (because, for the reason that) ....'

'To demonstrate (highlight, illustrate, support) his perspective (argument, opinion, stance, viewpoint) it would prove useful (helpful) to consider (employ, use, utilize) Y's study (investigation) in the following way (in a particular way).'

'For further confirmation (reinforcement, support, validation) of X's case (argument, opinion, stance, viewpoint) it would be useful (helpful) to cite the information (statistics) found in Y. The latter discovered (found, uncovered) evidence that...'

'A contrasting view (case, argument, opinion, stance, viewpoint) is that of...'

'Y modified (added to, built upon) X's research (hypothesis, study, research, theory, work) by...'

'However, (nevertheless,) this cannot be regarded as conclusive because research (in another study) by Y offered a different (an alternative, conflicting, opposing) viewpoint (perspective, theory). In Y's study, it was claimed (postulated) that...'

'A further (another) issue (point) relevant to this debate is...'

Phrases to use in Conclusions

'In outline (generally, ultimately) it appears that...'

'In answer (response) to the question...'

'By way of a final overview (answer) it is reasonable (fair, logical, possible) to state that...'

'In the final analysis...'

'In summary...'

SOCIOLOGICAL PERSPECTIVES

Definitions

Sociological Perspective: A broad approach, concerned with the aims and general principles governing Sociology as an academic discipline. It influences a Sociologist's choice of subject matter, theories and research methods. The main question it addresses is: *'How should we look at social occurrences?'*

Sociological Theory: A specific, coherent and evidenced-based explanation over why certain things happen within society. It is concerned with uncovering possible causal relationships. The main question it addresses is: *'Why is this happening?'*

Types of Sociological Theory:
1. Macro Theory looks at the large-scale behaviours of big Organizations, Institutions, Nation States and Major Global Developments.
2. Micro Theory looks at the small-scale interactions within Families, Tribes, Communities and other groups of limited size.

Types of Perspective

1. Logical Positivism

Definition: An approach which believes it possible to observe social life and establish reliable valid knowledge about <u>exactly</u> how it works

Founding Father: Augustus Comte (1798-1857)

Name Drops: Durkheim, Marx & Talcott Parsons

Assumption about Truth: The truth is *'out there'* and can be measured using scientific methods, *e.g.* observation

Core Belief: Sociology is a science

Main Focus: The gathering of social facts to uncover the laws which govern society and historical change

Attitude to Statistics: Statistics reflect real social facts and can be taken at face value

Type of Reasoning preferred: *'Deductive'* – theories are presented and tested against the facts

Derived Theories: The macro theories of *'Functionalism,' 'The New Right'* and *'Marxism'* – all of which emphasise the way social structure determines behaviour

Favoured Research Methods: *'Quantitative' e.g.* laboratory experiments and large-scale social surveys

Main Strength: Its systematic, data rich investigative procedures

Main Weakness: It's assumption that human behaviour can be equated with the reactions and movement of objects in the natural realm

Examples of Positivism in my Family History: the statistical survey of the census data of six Yorkshire settlements

2. Interpretivism (known also as anti-Positivism)

Definition: An approach emphasizing the various ways in which people interpret (or give meaning to) the world. How this affects their own participation in social and cultural life is also emphasised.

Founding Father: Max Weber (1864-1924)

Name Drops: Margaret Mead, George Ritzer & Erving Goffman

Assumption about Truth: Truth exists only in our heads and is constructed only through social interaction

Core Belief: Social action can best be understood by empathising with the way social actors perceive reality and the meaning they give to events and other people

Main Focus: Everyday life and its small-scale interactions

Attitude to Statistics: Sceptical; statistics are simply social constructs that don't necessarily reflect social reality

Type of Reasoning preferred: *'Inductive'* – facts are gathered first and then theories (firmly based upon the facts) are further developed

Derived Theories: The micro social action theories of *'Symbolic Interactionism,'* *'Phenomenology'* and *'Post Modernism,'* each of which stress how human interaction can create social structures

Favoured Research Methods: *'Qualitative' e.g.* participant observation and in-depth interviews

Main Strength: The stress upon the *'everyday world of action'* wherein people try to find meaning and agreement

Main Weakness: Its subjectivity and lack of ability to account for the influence of large-scale organizations

Examples of Interpretivism in my Family History: Shown in the reconstruction and interpretation of the religious beliefs of my ancestors

3. Critical Realism (known also as Realism)

Definition: An approach concerned with exposing the underlying (and often difficult to observe) processes, mechanisms and structures which govern society

Founding Father: Roy Bhaskar (1944-2014)

Name Drops: Anthony Giddens, Margaret Archer & Alex Callincos

Assumption about Truth: Truth is *'out there'* but difficult to perceive and measure with any degree of accuracy

Core Belief: Social behaviour is governed by hidden processes, mechanisms and structures that are difficult to uncover

Main Focus: The defence of rational scientific enquiry against *'Positivism'* and *'Post Modern'* challenges

Attitude to Statistics: Statistics need to be combined with other forms of data to provide meaningful information

Type of Reasoning preferred: *'Inductive'* at the beginning of a research project, then *'deductive'* as it progresses

Derived Theories: *'Basic Realism,'* *'Dialectical Realism'* & *'Meta-Realism'* (known also as *'Spiritual Realism'*)

Favoured Research Methods: A combination of *'quantitative'* and *'qualitative'* methods are favoured

Main Strength: It's ability to strike a balance between the naïve realism of *'Positivism'* and the subjectivity of *'Interpretivism'*

Main Weakness: Mostly suited to long-term a large investment of both time and money

Examples of Realism in my Family History: Discovering the cultural ideal of *'respectability'* as the main driving force behind the Smiths' strong work ethic

Conclusion

Sociology can be compared to a tree whose: -

1) Soil (nutrition) is Modern Western Civilization.

2) Roots are Western Materialism and Enlightenment Philosophy. (These *'roots'* emphasises the role of *'human reason'* as distinct from *'divine revelation'* as a means of obtaining knowledge).

3) Thick trunk is Sociology itself – itself sub-divided into the three main branches of:

3.1 *'Logical Positivism'* – divided again into the three smaller branches of: -
- Functionalism,
- New Right Theory
- Marxism

Hanging from these small branches are the twigs representing different *'quantitative'* research methods. Finally, any *'fruit'* hanging from the tree represent any useful data that result from employing those methods.

3.2 *'Interpretivism'* – divided again into the three smaller branches of: -
- Symbolic Interactionism
- Phenomenology
- Post Modernism.

Hanging from these small branches are the twigs representing different *'qualitative'* research methods. Finally, any *'fruit'* hanging from the tree represent any useful data that result from employing those methods.

3.3 *'Critical Realism'* – divided again into the three smaller branches of: -
- Basic Realism
- Dialectical Realism
- Meta-Realism

Hanging from these smaller branches are the twigs representing different *'quantitative'* and *'qualitative'* research methods. Finally, any *'fruit'* hanging from the tree represents any useful data resulting from the employment of those methods.

THE DIFFERENCE BETWEEN A *'SOUND'* AND AN *'UNSOUND'* THEORY

A **theory** is a combination of logically arranged ideas attempting to explain **why** certain relationships occur between different variables. A **variable** is any feature or relationship being measured.

Types of Theories: There are four types of theories: -
- **Analytical:** these are mathematically consistent but say little about social or scientific reality. Their chief value is in showing a logical consistency, *'String theory'* is an example.
- **Normative:** these are philosophically important in suggesting ethical codes of morality. Their chief value is in prescribing how behaviours within society ought to be. One example is the way *'belching after a meal'* is viewed as being good manners in some cultures and bad manners in others.
- **Metaphysical:** these presume that tangible relationships can exist between spiritual and natural phenomena. The supernatural is being able to influence the natural. One example is the belief that sickness or crop failures are caused by malignant spirits.
- **Scientific:** these are evidence based suggestions which attempt to explain why certain observable phenomena in the natural realm occur. They are open to both quantitative and qualitative verification, *e.g.* Einstein's theory of relativity.

The above types of theories may operate on a *'macro'* (large) or a *'micro'* (small) scale – attempting to explain *'much'* or *'little'* respectively. Within the Social Science area **macro theories** tend to be more difficult to verify.

The Characteristics of a Sound and an Unsound Theory

A sound theory is characterised by its:	An unsound theory is characterised by its:
Clear, precise expression	Poor, vague expression
Consistent use of appropriate terminology	Inconsistent use of difficult terminology
Clear explanation of underlying causes	Failure to explain underlying causes
Concise explanation of key facts	Muddled explanation of key facts
Accurate predictions	Inaccurate predictions
Openness to verification	Lack of openness to verification
Openness to amendment	Lack of openness to amendment
Justified conclusions, supported by valid and reliable evidence	Dogmatic assertions, having little basis in fact
Being <u>more</u> plausible than rival theories	Being <u>less</u> plausible than rival theories
Ability to generate further genuine ideas and pertinent research	Inability to generate further genuine ideas and pertinent research

Comments: A sound theory is not simply <u>descriptive</u> (*i.e.* recounting <u>what</u> happens), nor is it <u>prescriptive</u> (*i.e.* asserting what <u>should</u> happen); it's always <u>explanatory</u> (*i.e.* showing <u>why</u> things happen). It's also characterized by an attempt to close a gap in knowledge and by a sense of original thinking. A sound theory should always benefit (and even offer new insight into) a subject area.

Source: P. 32 Selfe L. P. (1987) *Advanced Sociology* Pan Study Aids, Pan (P/B) ISBN: 0-330-29552-7 REF: 301 SEL

THE STAGES OF QUESTIONNAIRE DESIGN

Questionnaire design is one of the most intricate of tasks, often requiring many drafts to arrive at the finished product. It is best achieved in the following stages: -

STAGE 1: Check the aims (terms of reference) of the Questionnaire. Decide which points need further probing. Consult (if need be) other interested parties, *i.e.* tutors, colleagues or the organisation who originally commissioned the research.

STAGE 2: Use a spider diagram and *'thought shower'* the points that need covering. Decide whether *'Liket Scales'* should be used to gain quantitative information.

STAGE 3: Delete any irrelevant points and place those remaining into a checklist.

STAGE 4: Convert each relevant point into a balanced mix of *'closed'* questions (that require a *'yes'* or *'no'* answer) and *'open-ended'* questions (that leave participants to give their own answers). Ensure teach question is <u>not</u>: -

- Abrupt or interrogative in nature (conveying an impression of rudeness)
- *'Double-barrelled'* – trying to ask too many questions all at once. (These are often revealed by the presence of the word *'and'*)
- Intrusive – dealing with highly personal matters, *e.g.* a person's sex life
- Irrelevant – they simply don't meet the terms of reference
- Badly expressed or worded in a highly-specialised way. However, the latter may be acceptable when surveying a specialised sample of people who *'know the jargon' i.e.* health professionals
- Patronising – *'talking down'* to the respondent
- Pleading – *'grovelling'* to the respondent *e.g. "Would you please, please, please answer these rather difficult questions?"*
- Presumptuous – guiding the respondent to an already predetermined answer *e.g. "Have you stopped smoking yet?"*
- Rambling – overlong and incoherent
- Deliberately *'tricky'* – trapping the respondent into giving answers they wouldn't normally divulge of their own free will. *"When did you stop having extra marital affairs?"*

STAGE 5: Design a standard but inviting *'Introduction'*

STAGE 6: Draft and redraft a *'trial questionnaire'* – take care to proof read it aloud and test it on friends and family. <u>Ensure all the terms of reference are fulfilled,</u> with a balanced mix of closed and open-ended questions.

STAGE 7: If required, draft out a *'Pilot Questionnaire'* and try it out on a carefully selected audience. (However, smaller surveys may <u>not</u> require either this or the next stage.)

STAGE 8: Check through the *'Pilot Questionnaire'* and note any: -
- Strengths and weaknesses in its design
- Areas where *'participant resistance'* or misunderstandings have occurred
- Further possible lines of enquiry
- Improvements that could be made

STAGE 9: Draft and redraft the final Questionnaire, proof reading it aloud between drafts. Check again that <u>all</u> its aims are being fulfilled. When doing this, decide whether to include any other lines of enquiry, and if so, add these questions to the draft. Employ computer spreadsheets and database packages to aid in the design of appropriate coding sheets (which categorise different types of answer using numbers or stock phrases).

STAGE 10: Begin using the Questionnaire when interviewing respondents. Make any personal introduction brief, factual and friendly.

STAGE 11: As part of the final Questionnaire make it very clear (in writing) that the respondent can withdraw their co-operation at any time should he (or she) wish to do so.

STAGE 12: Use coding sheets to tabulate results, checking they're **valid, reliable** and **representative (VRR).** Use appropriate computer graphics to aid in the presentation of results.

When conducting a survey, interviewers must <u>always comply</u> with the accepted professional criteria of being *'legal, decent, honest and truthful.'*

The *'Syllabus Summary Method'* (SSM)

Introduction

The **Syllabus Summary Method (SSM)** uses the objectives listed in a Syllabus as a basis for note-taking and learning. It also monitors a student's progress through simple number tallying, where: -

0 = Non-existent knowledge and understanding
1 = Very weak degree of knowledge and understanding
2 = Weak degree of knowledge and understanding
3 = Moderate degree of knowledge and understanding
4 = Strong degree of knowledge and understanding
5 = Very strong degree of knowledge and understanding
5* = Excellent (or outstanding) degree of knowledge and understanding

Stages

The **SSM** involves the following stages: -

1. Selecting a Topic to study *e.g.* Crime and Deviance

2. Reading around a Topic up to three times, using Syllabus notes and relevant textbook chapters or passages

3. Reading through any prepared notes (taken at lectures) up to three times on different days

4. Preparing **Syllabus Summary notes** by: -
- Breaking down the objectives of the Syllabus into component *'key'* points
- Basing sub-headings around those *'key'* points
- Following the *'number-name order.'* This *'numbers'* the key points and *'name drops'* key researchers. Look up the meaning of specialised terms like *'Dark Figure'* and note them down
- Citing a documentary source, recording the name, theoretical perspective and (if possible) the date of the source. Briefly (in one or two sentences) summing up the key idea or result
- Citing relevant Statistical Data (if any)
- Recording insightful thoughts or criticisms which spring naturally to mind

5. Checking personal progress (against the syllabus objectives) using the above tallying system and aiming for a score of **4/5**

Example of the SSM

Key

KT = Key term (to be looked up in a subject dictionary)

ND = *'Name drop'*

OT = Own thought, idea, criticism or question

A) Sociological explanations of Crime & Deviance: -

KT: *'Functionalism'*
- Functionalism
- Marxism
- Neo-Marxism
- Interactionism
- New Right

ND: - Durkheim

OT: - *"How does neo-Marxism differ from Marxism?"*

B) Crime figures

KT: - The *'Dark Figure'*
- The use of crime figures in analysing crime
- Problems in data gathering
- Problems in recording
- Problems in interpreting
- What crime figures show about major trends

ND: - Home Office Statistics

OT: - *"Home Office Statistics have problems with validity, reliability and representativeness due to insufficient collection and poor recording."*

Comments

For the **SSM** to work it's necessary to <u>follow clear syllabus guidelines</u> provided by the examination authority. Sadly, this is <u>not</u> always the case – such guidelines can sometimes be very ambiguous in content and poorly written in style. Should this be the case then the student can only do their best with the guidelines offered.

Ideally, using the **SSM** should produce notes which remain close to the original objectives (as outlined in the Syllabus).

REVISION AIDS 3: HIGHER LEVEL

Contents

1) Ethics in business

2) Financial statements

3) How best to interpret sources

4) The contrast between Modernism and Post-Modernism

5) The *'Dialectical Method'* of argumentation

6) The *'Fifteen Methods'* of verification

7) The *'Longsight Pathway'*

8) The role of Human Resources in workforce planning

BIBLIOGRAPHY

ETHICS IN BUSINESS

Business ethics (morally correct codes of conduct within this field) is of increasing importance due to the many rapid changes encountered within this Sector. More precise definitions are as follows: -

1) Ethics – the philosophical discipline concerned with establishing correct conduct amongst people on the small or large-scale. **Business ethics** seeks to establish right practice or custom in commerce. (The term *'ethics'* is derived from the Ancient Greek word *'ethos'* meaning *'custom'*).

2) Absolute (Universal) Standards – codes of conduct applicable to all people always, regardless of circumstances. They've often been summed up in the central commandments of the major world Faiths. However, at this present time (2013) much of the population in the Western World are following their own self-made standards (unrelated to any religious faith) or are simply accepting government direction or whatever the media deems as right.

3) Relative (Contingency) Standards – codes of conduct applicable to some people at set times and dependent upon circumstances, *i.e. 'belching'* after a meal is acceptable in some cultures but not in others. These standards are significant in the business world where greater effort is made to respect and show deference to another culture.

Self-Assessment Exercise

List five of the most common temptations in the Business world. Where did these temptations originate? Suggest ways in which they may be overcome. What may be the long-term results of unethical behaviour within a Business?

Part A: Types of Business Ethics

1. Ethical perspectives come in various forms: -
- **Absolutist** – ethical decisions based upon the belief that absolute standards of right and wrong do exist
- **Emotivist** – ethical decisions left entirely to the individual
- **Cultural** – ethical decisions determined by culture; what may be ethical in one culture is not so in another
- **Behaviourist** – ethical decisions based upon social pressure which may deliberately coerce behaviour into desired directions
- **Egotistical** – ethical decisions based upon the amount of pleasure they give
- **Utilitarian** – ethical decisions based upon what gives the most happiness to the greatest number of people.
- **Laissez-faire** – ethical decisions that are marginalised or playing no role at all in any business activity where profit maximisation is the sole goal
- **Pragmatic** – ethical decisions dependent upon immediate situational constraints *e.g.* what's accepted as right or wrong is dependent upon circumstances and may change as circumstances change.

2. Business ethics is not a new discipline and can be found in ancient sources, *i.e.* the Old and New Testaments of the Bible – with their instructions on how best to handle money, (Luke 16:9).

3. For individual employees, ethical business considerations may come to the fore when: -
- Competing for job promotions
- Recording expenses
- Making a difficult sale during times of economic recession
- Feeling pressurised to meet an impossible deadline
- Uncovering some form of abuse
- Approached by colleagues or the Manager to engage in something which is morally wrong
- Entertaining an important client
- Entertaining a genuine grievance against another party

4. For employers some of the above considerations also apply. However, further ethical business considerations arise when: -
- Forced to compete with other businesses in a stagnant market
- Advertising a new product whose sales appear to be falling
- Automating an old production line
- Making loyal employees redundant
- Confronting an employee's genuine grievance
- Disputing with a Trade Union
- Facing adverse publicity
- Engaged in a serious legal dispute with a major rival.

Part B: What Influences Ethical Behaviour in a Business?

Business ethics are influenced by all the factors that help change society, (listed in **CESSPITTS Analysis on p.145**).

1. The main *external* influences are: -
- The Media; secrets are more difficult to keep these days
- Pressure groups (these tend to stir up public opinion)
- The industry and its products – a Nuclear Power Plant would obviously need a strict ethical policy in health and safety
- Shifting cultural values
- The legal and regulatory environment

2. The main *internal* influences are: -
- The history of the Company; its original vision and traditions
- The current performance of the Company and the reputation it enjoys with outsiders.
- The effectiveness of internal communication and monitoring systems.
- Organisational structure – determining informal as well as formal controls over behaviour
- The decisions made and personal examples set by the Senior Management

Self-Assessment Exercise

Do you think that ethics should play any part in Business behaviour? To what extent, if any, do you think business behaviour in Britain is becoming more ethical? Give reasons for your answer.

Part C: What are the effects of Ethical Behaviour on a Business?

1. Good (or correct) ethical behaviour can <u>positively affect</u> a business by: -
- Providing stakeholder loyalty
- Reducing labour turnover
- Creating a positive public image
- Increasing sales – the feeling of belonging to *'a Company that is good to do business with'*
- Protecting against legal and non-legal problems (which could well have arisen due to poor or unethical behaviour)

2. Correct ethical behaviour may <u>negatively affect</u> a business by: -
- Incurring higher costs – leading to lower profit.
- Providing a conflict of aims, whereby financial goals clash with ethical aspirations
- Slower decision-making due to ethical considerations being considered
- Making it vulnerable to media-led charges of hypocrisy
- Allowing it to be taken advantage of by ruthless competitors

Self-Assessment Exercise

Describe how you make ethical decisions. What principles do you follow when making them?

FINANCIAL STATEMENTS

Definitions

Balance Sheet: The Balance Sheet is one of the Financial Statements that Limited Companies and PLCs produce each year for their Shareholders. It's a snapshot of the Company's financial situation at the year end, making its assets and liabilities known at that given moment in time. It's portrayed in two halves – the top half showing where the money is currently being used in the business (the net assets), and the bottom half showing where that money came from (the capital employed). To ensure consistency, the value of the two halves must be the same: **capital employed = net assets,** hence the term *'Balance Sheet.'*

Budget: An Expenditure Plan estimating the distribution of financial resources over the next financial period (usually one year). At the end of this period *'estimated expenditure'* is compared with *'actual expenditure'* and any difference between the two is known as a *'Variance.'*

Cash Flow: the record of an Organisation's income and expenditure in each period (from as short as a week to a year.)

Cash Flow Forecast: A projection of what a Company expects its cash income and expenditure to be in period (which can range from a week to a year).

Corporation Tax: A tax on a Firm's profits, charged as a percentage of those profits (this % may change from year to year).

Income Tax: Tax levied by the Government on wages, rent, interest and dividends. It's collected through a set of marginal rates, using income bands.

Revenue: The money received from the sale of output; not to be confused with **Profit,** which is the amount of revenue left after all costs have been deducted.

Trading Profit and Loss Account: This is a record of the Firm's trading activities over a previously defined period (whereas the Balance Sheet is the financial position at a given moment in time).

The **Profit and Loss Account** is an extended version of the **Trading Profit and Loss Account.** It looks at how well the Firm has traded over the period concerned (usually the last six months or one year). It also shows how much the Firm has earned from selling its product or service (its revenue) and how much it has paid out in costs (production costs, salaries etc.). The net difference between revenue and costs is the amount of **profit** earned or **loss** incurred.

Value Added Tax (VAT): A tax on the *'value added'* at each stage of production – on the difference between the value of the final goods, minus the cost of buying raw materials and intermediate goods. It's an *'Ad Valorem'* (per value) Tax because it represents a percentage of the selling price.

To find the latest tax rates it's best to consult relevant web site sources, (which can change over time.)

BALANCE SHEET– EXAMPLE

FIXED ASSETS (FA)
+ Land
+ Property, premises and freehold buildings
+ Machinery
+ Furniture and fittings
+ Vehicles (or motor van) account
- Depreciation (may not always be included)
= Total Fixed Assets

LONG TERM ASSETS) (is often classified as belonging to the fixed asset category)
+ Long term investments (may be included as a fixed asset that can't be cashed within a year))

CURRENT ASSETS (CA)
+ Closing stock (latest recorded stock date)
+ Debtors (including loans to friends)
- Bad debts
+ Cash in hand (including current bank balance)
+ Payment made in advance (often to cover bills and insurance)
+ Rent due
+ Current and short term investments
= Total Current Assets

INTANGIBLE ASSETS (IA) (Non-physical assets that are often difficult to estimate)
+ Goodwill *e.g.* Company contacts and reputation
+ Intellectual Property *E.g.* Patents, Licenses and Trade Marks
= Total intangible assets

LONG TERM LIABILITIES (Due in more than a year)
+ Long term debt
+ Mortgages
+ Deferred tax
= Total Long Term Liabilities

CURRENT LIABILITIES (CL) (Due in less than a year)
+ Creditors (including loans from friends)
+ Accrued expenses (including unpaid bills)
+ Bank or Building Society overdrafts **(BO)**
+ Advance payment to the Company
+ Bills for machinery
+ Dividends due to shareholders
+ Current taxation
= Total Current Liabilities

OTHER LIABILITIES
+ Capital
+ Net profit
- Drawings (money taken out to meet immediate needs)
= Total Other Liabilities

Capital employed: (CE) = FA + CA – CL (-BO)

Net assets: (NA) = FA + CA – CL

Working capital: (WC) = CA - CL

TRADING PROFIT AND LOSS ACCOUNT – EXAMPLE

Revenue

+ Sales cash
+ Sales credit
+ Rent received
+ Income from investments
+ Grants, gifts and bequests

= Total Income, Revenue, or Sales Turnover

- **Cost of goods sold (or cost of sales)** = + opening stock (earliest recorded stock date)
  + Purchases
  + Cost of goods made
  + Carriage and postage
  - Returns (purchased returns account)
  - Closing stock

= Gross Profit

- **Total Expenses** = + Wages (Salaries account)
  + Rent and rates
  + Lighting and heating
  + Sundries and petty cash
  + Selling, distribution and promotion
  + Motoring and transport
  + Repairs and maintenance
  + Bank charges
  + Telephone
  + ICT and electronic communication
  + Stationary, printing and photocopying
  + Insurance
  + Bad, irrecoverable and *'doubtful'* debts
  + Depreciation
  - Advanced payments

= Net Profit before Taxation

- Government taxation

= Net Profit earned for Shareholders

- Dividends paid to shareholders
- Personal drawings by owners
+ Profit carried forward from previous Accounting Period

= Retained Profit

This is the profit available to be ploughed back into the business (or to be carried forward into the next Accounting Period). Total income (**Y**) minus all expenses (**X**) (including cost of goods sold) gives total profit or loss (**P/L**). Hence, **Y - X = P/L.**

Key

+ Add
- Subtract

HOW BEST TO INTERPRET SOURCES?

Introductory Comment

In both History and Social Science, students need to evaluate and interpret a whole variety of information sources. (A *'source'* is any evidence which needs to be interpreted; *i.e.* Business Case Studies. Data response questions, exam comprehensions, historical documents and statistical tables.)

The art of interpretation is technically called *'Hermeneutics.'* It derives from the Greek verb *'Hermeneuo,'* meaning *'to interpret in an organized and systematic way.'*

A source's *'context'* refers to its environment (the setting) in which it was produced. The following *'steps'* are most helpful when interpreting a source: -

Step 1: Discern the Type of Source

To discern (work out) a source the student must decide whether it's: -

1) Clear or Unclear: Clear sources *i.e.* a Business Memorandum may be taken at face value – *'what you see is what you get.'* In contrast, unclear sources *e.g.* a shard of pottery bearing an ancient language may require more elaborate methods of interpretation.

2) Complete or Fragmentary: A complete source *e.g.* a Psychological Case Study which contains all the necessary information in one document. In contrast, a fragmentary source is the above shard of pottery, providing an incomplete body of information. Fragmentation is especially acute with Ancient documents; *e.g.* *'The Dead Sea Scrolls'* (many of which are nearly disintegrated with age).

3) Contemporary (written around the time of the events in question) or Non-contemporary (written either a short or a long time after the events in question). Contemporary documents convey a sense of immediacy (though often fall short of giving a wider picture of events). Written during the Second World War, *'The Diaries of Ann Frank'* could hardly be relied upon to give a comprehensive picture of the Holocaust even though they were written by one of its most famous victims. They provide an immediate portrayal of the horrors of the time.

In contrast, non-contemporary sources may be able to offer a more long-term view and give access to a broader range of information. A case in point would be a Multi-Volume History of the Second World War. However, on a cautionary note, non-contemporary sources may attempt to justify earlier conduct *e.g.* political memoirs written by disgraced politicians like former **President Nixon.** In such cases evidence, may be twisted to cast the author in a more favourable light.

4) Internal or External to a culture or organisation; *e.g.* *'The Washington Post'* news reports of the scandals surrounding **President Clinton** in **1998** would be an internal cultural source. In contrast, an **Egyptian** news report on the same issue would be an external cultural source, outside of American Society.

5) Mono or Multi-genre – where the source is presented in only one (mono) way, *e.g.* **a list of safety instructions.** In contrast, **The Bible** combines a multiplicity of genres, ranging from the poetry of *'Psalms'* through to the formal theological treatise of *'Paul's letter to the Romans.'* Multi-genre material needs a more elaborate interpretative methodology.

6) <u>Official</u> or <u>Unofficial</u> – Does the source material derive from a government or non-government source? A **tax demand** is a government (official) document, whilst an **anarchist party leaflet** would constitute a non-government (unofficial) piece of literature. Most *'official'* documents tend to represent one viewpoint – that of the government. In contrast, unofficial documents often represent a considerable diversity of viewpoints.

7) <u>Quantitative</u> or <u>Qualitative</u>. Does the source convey quantitative (numeric or statistical) information using charts, graphs and tables *e.g.* Crime Figures or Census Returns? Or does it instead convey qualitative (non-numeric or non-statistical) information *e.g.* an artefact like a shard of pottery or wall graffiti alleging that *'all Police are thieves?'*

8) <u>Verbal</u> or <u>visual</u>. Does the source speak mainly through (verbal) words or through (visual) pictures? In practice, many documents *i.e.* **newspaper extracts** combine both verbal and visual material.

Step 2: Discover as much as Possible about the Source's *'context'*

1) To discover a source's context involves using *'the five Ws: -'*
- *When* was, a source written?
- *Where* was, it written?
- *Who* wrote it?
- *What* was written in it?
- *Why* was it written?

2) Once the available facts about a source have been established the following *'Contexts'* need to be assessed: -
- **The personal (psychological) context:** The writer's probable state of mind when completing the document – his abilities, health, intentions, motives, degree of truthfulness and general sense of well-being
- **The literary (grammatical) context:** The wording used in the source – the writer's use of grammar and the genre (types of literature) employed
- **The social (peer group) context:** The writer's own position in society – his family relationships, likely peer groups, resource constraints and the immediate audience being addressed by the document
- **The cultural (historical) context:** The dominant attitudes, beliefs and ideas found within the writer's contemporary culture. These would include artistic, economic and technical development, the prevalent government system and any degree of social unrest
- **The physical (geographical) context:** The general geography of the location in which the document was written (or found) and the strength of materials used in its assembly, *e.g.* Egyptian papyrus found on an Ancient Egyptian rubbish dump

3) Special note must be taken of a source's internal relationships where one occurrence has a marked effect upon another *e.g.*
- **A positive causal relationship** – where an increase in **x** will cause an increase in **y**. (and any decrease in **x** will cause a decrease in **y** *e.g.* the growth seen in such staple industries as coal (**x**) led to an increase in steel production (**y**) in early nineteenth century Britain
- **An inverse causal relationship** – where an increase in **x** will cause a decrease in **y**. Conversely, any decrease in **x** will cause an increase in **y** *e.g.* the growth in Roman power (**x**) caused a reduction in the power of Carthage (**y**)
- **A null causal relationship** – where changes in **x** or **y** are largely unrelated to each other *e.g.* the Thirty Years War in early modern Europe (**x**) and the concurrent rise of the Manchu Dynasty (**y**) in China.
- **A co-relationship** – where **x** and **y** occur together directly as the result of another totally unrelated cause (**z**) *e.g.* the First World War (**z**) facilitated the rise of Irish Fascism (**x**) and

the rise of Japanese Imperialism (**y**). No causal relationship existed between **x** and **y**; rather it's a case of **z** having created the conditions for both *x* and *y* to exist simultaneously.

Step 3: Become familiar with the various problems which may arise within any Source

A variety of problems may well exist within any source, including: -

1) General problems – noted by the mnemonic (memory term) **VRR** for **V**alidity, **R**eliability and **R**epresentativeness. Is the given source document: -
- **Valid**? Is it genuine and not a forgery? Is it accurate, truthful to the facts and relevant to the research question? Does it adequately cover the area under scrutiny? Can it be used to support or nullify any conclusion?
- **Reliable?** Can its contents be confirmed by other documentary, historical, scientific or archaeological evidence?
- **Representative?** Is it typical of the other documents produced in its contemporary society or a group within that society?

2) Specific problems including: -
- **Alien ways of thinking:** The cultural attitudes, beliefs and ways of thinking present within a piece of evidence may be alien to students studying it; *e.g.* the letters of **Tsar Nicholas II.** These contain the thoughts of a rather unintelligent late nineteenth century Russian autocrat, unduly influenced by medieval ideas of monarchical government and the Russian Orthodox Church. These are hardly *'familiar ways'* of thinking to a modern teenage **'A'** level History student, living in the age of the Internet.
- **Bias:** The source may be overtly prejudiced in favour of (or against) a particular idea, person, group or situation; *e.g.* the Fourth Century Church Historian **Eusebius'** bias in favour of the Emperor Constantine amounted to fawning flattery.
- **Confusion:** The source may be very confused, inarticulate or needlessly verbose; *e.g.* The speeches given by the First World War General **Douglas Haig** were often comical in this respect. In a speech, (presumably given following an army sports demonstration), he was once alleged to have told the troops, *"I hope that you will run equally well in front of the enemy."*
- **Conflicting interpretations:** one example being the debate which almost always follows an improvement in **'A'** level or **'GCSE'** results. Some commentators attribute an improvement to a more effective performance of the educational system. Other equally well-qualified commentators allege that falling marking standards were the real cause of this apparent improvement.
- **Deliberate deception:** Those who produced the source may be liars, deliberately trying to hide their actions. Soft words (euphemisms) may be employed to disguise ugly realities; *e.g.* the Nazi regime used the euphemism *'resettlement'* in place of *'extermination'* when planning to destroy the Jewish people during World War Two.
- **Discrepancies:** where equally good sources may contradict one another. It may be unclear whether such a conflict is only *'apparent'* (due to a lack of sources that could offer reconciling evidence), or whether there is indeed an actual and serious contradiction. In the latter instance, it would be necessary to prefer one source over another and to give reasons for this. Juries are often called upon to assess conflicting pieces of evidence during a major criminal trial.
- **Fragmentary evidence:** there may be a lack of other evidence to support (or nullify) the claims of a source. Particularly in Ancient History the evidence may simply not be there to validate or discredit a claim; *e.g.* many of the victories recorded on Ancient Egyptian royal inscriptions may have been real or they may have been fabricated for internal propaganda purposes. Some of the inscriptions have no corroborating evidence. There is simply no

way of finding out the truth.

- **Linguistic difficulties:** the source may be in a language that is either impossible or very difficult to translate; *e.g.* a certain Eskimo dialect is reputed to have thirty words corresponding to the one English word for *'snow.'* The linguistic nightmare this would cause to translators can be easily imagined.

3) Students tend to bring their own personal agendas, ideas and prejudices to bear when approaching a source. They're also likely to be under a great deal of academic and personal pressure. Such factors may cause students to overlook important information or to *'read into'* sources things which may not actually be there.

Step 4: Use Relevant Methods for Dealing with Source Problems

To resolve (or reduce) problems in source interpretation the student must: -

1) Decide whether <u>one</u> or <u>both</u> following *'levels of interpretation'* should be used: -
- **The literal level:** where the document is taken at its *'face value,'* accepting that *'it says what it means.'* This is often a good starting point and is useful with the simpler, more straightforward sources. However, it can be shallow and prove inefficient in getting to the heart of a more complicated document *e.g.* a highly symbolic poem.
- **The underlying level:** where the less obvious (covert) meaning of a document is explored. It's often a good generator of ideas and is useful with less straightforward sources. However, it can be highly subjective, leading the student to *'read into'* the source things which simply aren't there. Its use with factual reports would be especially limited.

It's crucially important to make a clear distinction between *'exegesis'* (<u>reading out</u> of a source items of information which already exist within it) and *'eisegesis,'* (<u>reading into</u> a source one's own biased ideas, or items of information which really have no bearing upon it at all). The former approach is to be wholeheartedly practised and the latter totally avoided.

2) Examine any *'cause and effect'* relationships. When doing this it's important to: -
- Briefly describe the causes being uncovered.
- List the causes in order of ascending or descending importance.
- Evaluate whether the causes are **complementary** or **conflicting.**
- Justify and summarise the evaluation <u>using the available evidence.</u>

3) Employ a <u>quantitative approach,</u> using as many sources as possible to build up a larger picture of events and their setting. This should then be followed by a <u>qualitative approach</u> which prioritises the sources. In project work, simpler sources are best selected first, followed by those of a more complex nature. In addition, always look out for any possible connections between different sources.

4) Follow an interdisciplinary approach – where proven theories and methods (taken from a variety of social science subjects) are used to *'tease out'* the true meaning of a source. The theoretical approach being brought to bear upon a source should be stated and its use justified; *e.g. 'structuralism',* (that believes social structures are the main determinant of behaviour) because it provides the most plausible explanation of a in society. Ideally <u>more than one theoretical approach</u> needs to be used and justified. In most Social Science or Business Studies essays different theoretical approaches are used when examining a social issue, e.g. Functionalist analysis may be combined with Marxist theory when exploring the role of education in society.

5) Adapt the method of interpretation to the type of source being studied. Some sources (like statistical items) can be interpreted in a logical step-by-step manner. However, others (like a

medieval folk tale) would require a far more intuitive approach. The student's own creative imagination could be brought to bear when trying to reconstruct the feelings which the medieval tale may have aroused at the time of its first telling.

6) Never rely upon one single method of interpretation. Using a selection of pertinent methods would increase marks in any examination. A source is often better understood when a student tries to summarise it in his/her own words.

Conclusion

Although **Steps 1-4** amount to little more than common sense, Examination Boards still require students to display both subject knowledge and a flexibility of approach in the interpretation of sources. A thorough application of these four steps will enhance project and exam work. Furthermore, interpretative skills such as these are just as applicable in areas like Journalism and Business Administration. Using them encourages the critical thinking needed to spot bogus stories or mistakes in either content or presentation.

To assist source interpretation, it's sometimes helpful to employ the simple schemes found in some Advanced Level Text books, *e.g.* **POPS: -**

- Province – *'where does the source come from?'*

- Origin – *'who wrote the source?'*

- Purpose – *'why was it written?'*

- Style – *'What style was it written in?'*

Another example is **TRUCC: -**

- Typicality – *'How typical (or representative) is the source?'*

- Reliability – *'Is the source reinforced by other relevant and credible information?'*

- Utility – *'How useful is the source in answering a set question (or in meeting the terms of reference of a particular project)?'*

- Comprehensibility – *'How easy is the source to understand?'*

- Comparison – *'How does this source compare with other sources in terms of TRUCC?'*

In answering a question it's sometimes helpful to use **POPS** first and then **TRUCC.**

THE CONTRAST BETWEEN MODERNISM AND POST- MODERNISM

Modernism is characterised by a belief in: -

1. A world-view (**paradigm**) based upon materialism
2. Objective standards of right and wrong
3. Secular-based confidence that *'Man'* or *'Science'* has all the answers
4. The ability of *'Big ideas'* to change the world, *i.e.* as promised in Socialism and Nationalism (which attempt to permeate into and to change every aspect of society)
5. Progress toward a man-made utopia with no reference to supernatural beliefs or intervention
6. The importance of structure, logical thinking and the use of scientific methodology
7. The ability of language to reflect and correspond to reality
8. The ability of the human intellect (or reason) to act as the sole source of knowledge
9. The ability of science and large-scale government action to solve most major problems in society
10. The responsibility of the State (and hierarchical bureaucracy) to order human affairs
11. A *'collective'* rather than an *'individual'* identity. Group loyalties, based upon race or class are viewed as long term, often spanning successive generations
12. The idea that identities are largely determined at birth or by impersonal socio-economic forces
13. Distinct sexual male and female identities
14. Its own right to act as a dominant ideology, demanding a total commitment – whilst persecuting other belief systems (A person's first loyalty is to a political party representing the Nation or to some other form of ideology)
15. The ideal that the highest goal in life is service to the State or to Humanity in general. (Marxism was perhaps the most extreme example of Modernism)

Post-Modernism is characterised by a belief in: -

1. A world-view (**paradigm**) based upon scepticism
2. An individual's ability to create his/her own values of right and wrong
3. The sceptical view that there are no big answers to life's questions and dilemmas
4. The view that no *'big ideas'* can change the world. Change, (where it does take place at all) will be through networking with like-minded people and with pressure groups working on a local level
5. A desire to find some form of *'do it yourself'* spirituality that will bring personal fulfilment
6. A growing integration between *'low brow'* (popular) and *'highbrow'* (elite) arts with a critical stance taken toward science and technology
7. The value of emotion, free-flow creativity, divergent thinking and the *'deconstruction of language'*
8. Personal experience and intuition being the sole (or major sources) of knowledge
9. The inability of science (or large-scale government) to permanently solve any major problems
10. The capacity of smaller, *'user-friendly'* non-government organisations to better order human affairs
11. Individual rather than group identity. Group loyalties are viewed as weak and changeable, operating only on a short-term basis. People's first loyalty is to themselves and their family.
12. The idea that identities can be self-created and changed through *'lifestyle choices'*
13. A blurring of male and female sexual identity
14. Multi-culturalism *i.e.* a plurality of diverse beliefs is accepted and recognised as being equally valid.

15. The highest goal in life is self-satisfaction. (The *'New Age Movement'* is perhaps the best example of Post-Modernism)

The Strengths of Post-Modernism include its: -
1. Stimulation of linguistic studies and its ability to see how language can be misused for propaganda purposes
2. Suspicion of hierarchical figures claiming *'unique accessibility'* to some form of *'absolute truth'*
3. Scepticism concerning certain other ideologies *i.e.* which promise to have all the answers to life
4. Critical hostility toward mass advertising

The Weaknesses of Post-Modernism include its: -
1. Roots in the philosophically flawed system of *'Marxist Existentialism'*
2. Tendency to deny the ability of language to point to any kind of objective reality
3. Near incomprehensible and intellectually pretentious jargon. This poses the question *'What is the real nature of Post-Modernism?'*
4. Tendency toward a wide-ranging scepticism, leading to an inevitable undermining of any legal, religious and scientific system. It uses language to suggest that language itself has no real meaning
5. Tendency to break down the important (and needful) distinction between reality and fantasy
6. Inability to see that people have an instinctive need to find *'big answers'* to life's dilemmas

Currently (2013) there's a rather indecisive debate as to whether **Post-Modernism** is a continuation of **Modernism** or whether it exists as a new phenomenon. Thinkers like **Zygmunt Bauman** draw a contrast between an old, dogmatic, highly exclusive, *'solid'* modernity and a new, highly inclusive ambivalent *'liquid'* modernity, (the latter is the equivalent of **Post-Modernism** today).

Since the early 1970s, there's been a major cultural shift toward **Post-Modernism,** especially in the Arts and Humanities. However, many of the economic and political structures and urban settlement patterns associated with **Modernism** remain in place. There has not yet been the major structural break that took place when **Traditional Societies** became **Modern Societies** following the beginning of the Industrial Revolution during the late eighteenth century. Also, **Modernism** still appears to be dominant in the natural sciences. If a real shift from a **Modern** to a **Post-Modern** Society is happening, then it's still at an early stage and progress has been very patchy.

THE *'DIALECTICAL METHOD'* OF ARGUMENTATION

The dialectical method of argumentation is best used when presenting detailed arguments containing different points of view. It's often used at postgraduate level in higher academic disciplines like Philosophy and tends to follow a logical structure: -

Step 1: The asking of a general question in a clearly-defined area of knowledge
⇓
Step 2: The division of the general question into a series of sub-questions
⇓
Step 3: A brief decisive answer to each of the sub-questions (This constitutes the *'Thesis'* or original answer)
⇓
Step 4: A numbered list of arguments in favour of this original answer
⇓
Step 5: A brief opposing answer to each of the sub-questions found in *'Step Two'* (The *'Antithesis'* or opposing answer)
⇓
Step 6: A numbered list of arguments in favour of this opposing answer
⇓
Step 7: A general response to first the *'Thesis'* and then the *'Antithesis'*
⇓
Step 8: The presentation of any original ideas and thoughts, (taken and cited from a variety of sources)
⇓
Step 9: A numbered list of arguments answering those put forward in *'Step 4'* to remove any objections
⇓
Step 10: Closing Comments and the final answer given to the sub-questions (in *'Step 2'*). Consideration is also given to any practical applications

N.B: The numbered arguments in *'Step 9'* should equal those in *'Step 4.'*

Comments

The above *'Steps'* represent an application of an *'antithetic dialectic,'* which assumes that no reconciliation can occur between the *'Thesis'* and *'Antithesis.'* One or the other must be chosen. It is a case of *'either/or'* rather than *'and/both.'*

Some variation and simplification of this method can be used, based upon the structure followed by the medieval thinker Thomas Aquinas (1225-1274).

Following *'Step Seven,'* this variation involves attempting to establish a *'Synthesis'* (reconciling answer) of the *'Thesis'* with the *'Antithesis.'* For example: -

Step 8: Original ideas are presented providing a fresh answer to the sub-questions. This serves to reconcile the *'Thesis'* and *'Antithesis'* in the *'Synthesis'* or reconciling answer
⇓
Step 9: A numbered list of arguments answers those put forward in *'Step 4,'* each in favour of a new *'Synthesis'*
⇓
Step 10: Brief Closing Comments – with a final reconciling answer given to the original question

The above steps represent an application of a *'synthetic dialectic'* which assumes that reconciliation can occur between the *'Thesis'* and *'Antithesis.'* Each is viewed as being to some degree right; it's a case of *'and/both'* rather than *'either/or.'*

Such a *'synthetic dialectic'* can delineate and consider both sides of an argument, acting as a useful planning tool – especially for long pieces of work. Its weakness lies in its own rigidity and tendency to cramp spontaneous thought. Consequently, it's best employed after a freethinking *'thought shower.'* For dialectical reasoning to succeed it's needful to begin the whole process with an open mind – one not already decided upon a pre-determined answer. It needs also to be related to everyday life – otherwise it would be nothing more than an irrelevant intellectual exercise.

THE *'FIFTEEN METHODS'* OF VERIFICATION

Verification is the organized process of testing, confirming (or refuting) claims, hypotheses, ideas and theories. It facilitates the process of learning. Up to fifteen methods (tests) of verification can be employed at any one time to confirm the validity (truthfulness) of a statement. The statement itself could be anything at all *i.e.* an opinion, scientific finding, theory or philosophy. The methods are:

1) THE CLARITY TEST – examines whether a statement (or theory) is being presented in a clear and lucid fashion. This test is especially pertinent in relation to damaged ancient documents, *e.g.* the two surviving manuscripts of the Roman Historian Tacitus. Stated briefly, the *'Clarity Test'* asks, *"Is it sufficiently clear to be worth examining?"*

2) THE COHERENCE TEST – examines whether a statement (or theory) is logically sound and follows a clear line of reasoning. It consists of: -
   a) **An Assumption:** *an often-unexpressed belief (or presupposition) that forms the basis of an openly stated belief, idea, opinion or conclusion, e.g.* the belief that the rise of Information Technology will increase business profitability
   b) **A Deduction:** *an openly stated belief, idea or opinion based upon the assumption, e.g.* the view that there needs to be a substantial investment in new Information Technology equipment aimed at increasing business profitability.

   c) **A Conclusion:** *the final evaluation (reasoned opinion) that draws upon any available information (as well as from the previous assumption and deduction,) e.g.* the suggestion that **20%** of the next annual budget will be needed to invest in purchasing new Information Technology equipment (to increase business profitability).

   d) **Application:** *the practical outworking (application) of a reasoned opinion (conclusion) in daily life, e.g.* the purchase and installation of brand new Information Technology equipment (to increase business profitability).

Briefly, the *'Coherence Test'* asks, *"Is it logical, e.g. do the different parts of an argument (or theory) cohere together?"*

3) THE CONFORMITY TO AN EXTERNAL STANDARD TEST – examines whether a statement or theory fully conforms to a recognised external standard. This could be a government regulation, legal requirement, health and safety standard, agreed professional code of conduct or syllabus requirement. Briefly, the *'Conformity Test'* asks, *"Does it conform to an objective standard, laid down by a recognised external authority?"*

4) THE DENIAL TEST – examines the consequences that arise when a statement (or theory) is denied, ignored or misunderstood. An example was the denial by some Doctors that the high death rates within certain nineteenth century maternity wards were due to poor personal hygiene by medical staff. The consequence of this was an unnecessary loss of life amongst expectant and nursing mothers. Briefly, the *'Denial Method'* asks, *"What are the consequences of denying it?"*

5) THE EVIDENTIAL TEST – examines whether a statement (or theory) is supported (or refuted) by relevant quantitative or qualitative external evidence. For example, in astronomy, possible external evidence supporting the view that the universe will continue to expand indefinitely is the **20%** higher than expected speed at which Super Nova (large exploding stars) are moving away from each other. Briefly, the *'evidential test'* asks, *"What evidence exists to support (or refute) it?"*

6) THE EXPLANATORY TEST – examines whether a statement (or theory) adequately explains a specific occurrence; *e.g.* in Sociology the theory of *'Structural Functionalism'* successfully explains the presence of social stability, but provides only a poor explanation of social conflict. Briefly, the *'explanatory test'* asks, *"How much does it adequately explain?"*

7) THE FALSIFICATION TEST – examines whether a statement (or theory) can be falsified (disproved). If a claim cannot be totally disproved, then it's difficult to decide whether to accept or reject it. All that remains is an unverifiable speculation rather than a testable theory, *e.g.* the claim that intelligent life exists in another Universe. Briefly, the *'falsification test'* asks, *"Can it be disproved?"*

8) THE LINGUISTIC TEST – examines whether *'key words'* in a particular statement (or theory) can be clearly defined and used in a consistent way. For example, in a Business Report the word *'Capital'* could be used in a variety of misleading ways unless care is taken to clearly define its usage. Briefly, the *'linguistic test'* asks, *"Are key words clearly defined and consistently used?"*

9) THE OPTIONAL TEST – examines the credibility of a statement (or theory) by assessing whether there are any alternatives. Briefly, the *'optional test'* asks, *"Are there any better alternatives?"* (Should the alternatives have worse problems than the original statement (or theory) would be more credible.)

10) THE PRACTICAL BENEFIT TEST – examines whether a statement (or theory) offers practical benefit to others; *e.g.* a new approach in counselling may help social workers to: -
• Show more patience with emotionally troubled clients.
• Increase the level of empathy with clients suffering from learning difficulties.
Briefly, the *'practical benefit'* test asks, *"Does it benefit others?"*

11) THE PRAGMATIC TEST – examines whether a statement (or theory) achieves relevant objectives; *e.g.* a new technique of *'client servicing'* may well lead to the fulfilment of Sales Targets. Briefly, the *'pragmatic test'* asks, *"Does it achieve its goals?"*

12) THE PREDICTABILITY TEST – examines whether a statement or theory successfully forecasts carefully selected future events. For example, Einstein's Theory of Relativity received greater credibility when it successfully predicted that heavy gravity objects would bend the light rays of distant stars. In contrast, Economics' constant failure to successfully predict anything other than strictly short-term events has lowered the status of this subject. Briefly, the *'predictability test'* asks, *"Can it successfully forecast future events?"*

13) THE REINFORCEMENT TEST – examines whether a statement (or theory) reinforces (gives greater credence to) a given area of knowledge by making a unique contribution to it. For example, the theories of Skinner reinforced the discipline of Psychology by: -

- Showing the importance of environmental factors in determining behaviour.
- Implying the possibility that *'social conditioning'* may serve to improve behaviour.

Briefly, the *'reinforcement test'* asks, *"Does it reinforce (or contribute to) the advancement of knowledge?"*

14) THE RELIABILITY TEST – examines whether, under similar conditions, the same statement (or theory), when being tested, produces the same results; *e.g.* a computer can only be viewed as being reliable if it obtains the same results from the same amount of data given on different occasions. Briefly, the *'reliability test'* asks, *"Can the same results be obtained at different periods of time?"*

15) THE REPRESENTATIVE TEST – examines whether a statement (or theory) is typical (representative) of a larger body of information; *e.g.* any sample of people used in a social survey must be *'representative'* of the wider population. Briefly, the *'representative test'* asks, *"How typical is it?"*

Although all the above tests cannot guarantee absolute certainty, they do, when taken together, strongly reinforce the credibility of a statement (or theory). The strengths of each of these tests lie in their: -

- Helpfulness in decision-making and evaluation
- Ability to produce greater clarification of thought, especially when working under pressure
- Capacity to aid the learning process
- Flexibility – where different tests are used in different combinations to assess a statement (in both the personal and professional fields)
- Potential to reinforce an argument, either in defence of, or against a case
- Capacity to check an *'intuitive feeling'* about some matter or problem
- Usefulness (at an early stage) in exposing bogus claims, weak ideas, poor decision-making and flawed reasoning. Their use greatly lessens the risk of being fooled by others

However, certain weaknesses are inherent to these tests, including their: -

- Inability to act as a cure-all for personal or organisational apathy
- Dependence upon a *'key figure,'* to actively implement them within an organisation
- tendency to transform a user into a clever *'know it all'* (unless handled wisely)
- Need for at least three of the methods to arrive at a stronger overall conclusion
- Dependence upon the *'user'* who is responsible for choosing the most pertinent method(s) to suit a situation

Despite the above weaknesses these tests are invaluable when problem-solving or decision-making. Their use enhances evaluation skills whilst sharply reducing the risk of serious misjudgements. For those who are willing and open minded they represent fifteen useful keys to very effective evaluation within a whole variety of assignments. Pertinent ones must always be used in any detailed evaluation.

THE LONGSIGHT PATHWAY

This Pathway was first drafted on Monday, the First of December 2003, at *'Longsight Public Library'* in Manchester, U.K. (before setting off to engage GCSE English Private Tuition)

Introduction

The *'Longsight Pathway'* is the path along which an **idea** must travel to gain popular acceptance. An idea's movement forward along *'the pathway'* can be a very uncertain and hazardous process. The pathway may be littered with various obstacles, each having the capacity to seriously weaken (or deflect) the original idea. Should it *'hit'* an obstacle or veer down a blind alley then the outcome could well be total rejection, or at the very least, a weakening of its impact. To gain popular acceptance an idea <u>must</u> overcome (or successfully negotiate) these obstacles - its very existence depends upon it. (Please note that the word *'idea'* is used in its broadest sense, covering any original concept, *i.e.* from fashion to science.)

As it travels **The Longsight Pathway** an idea passes through four major *'phases'* – each comprising of smaller *'stages'*: -
'Conception' – where the idea has its beginnings in terms of speculative thought and creativity
'Testing Phase' – where the idea is verified and assessed
'Manufacture' – where the idea is turned into a product and thrust onto the Market
'Acceptance' – where the idea becomes embedded within society and accepted as part of the culture (however – as the vagaries of fashion clearly show – this may <u>not</u> be a long-term acceptance!)

An idea can fail at any stage – even <u>after</u> having enjoyed a period of social acceptance. Different reasons are given for its *'Failed Development'* and subsequent rejection in the Public Domain (please see **p.183**).

The **Longsight Pathway** suggests that, in the long term, any new idea faces three possible outcomes: -
- **Social rejection** – the idea is not accepted but is dropped and quickly forgotten
- **Small group acceptance** – the idea is accepted by a small sub-culture
- **Social acceptance** – the idea is accepted within the wider Public Domain where it may last for a short (or long) time.

The history of failed inventions has shown that very few ideas make it to the third outcome. An idea's success often results from the efforts of many, (mostly anonymous) people. These days' team work by specialists from widely different academic backgrounds is needed to guide an idea along the *'Longsight Pathway.'* The days of the lone genius being able to do everything are long over (and perhaps never really existed in the first instance).

The **Longsight Pathway** may give the impression that an idea succeeds by simply following a sequential course from one small stage to another, negotiating any hindrances along the way. However in reality, things are far often more complicated because: -

1) The **Pathway** is concerned <u>only</u> with the popular (social) acceptance of an idea itself, <u>not</u> whether the idea is correct or false, good or bad. False ideas can just as readily gain public acceptance – especially when *'wrapped'* in an attractive guise *i.e.* a scientific theory, (as with **Social Darwinism** which helped legitimize Nazi atrocities).

2) It may be used to trace the progress of ideas in areas as diverse as religion, science and fashion. The *'Pathway'* also can be applied in many cultures and nations.

3) The complexity of an idea may mean that, at best, it will attain only a sub-social acceptance, *e.g.* **Quantum Theory** (widely accepted amongst physicists) but not yet enjoying the same popular acceptance as Einstein's **Theory of Relativity**). Others (like the discovery of the **Higgs Bosom** in **July 2012**) may be accompanied by a flurry of publicity and then forgotten by the world at large until it becomes useful in some practical application.

4) The ideas themselves may *'leap'* across several stages (known as the *'Longsight Leap'*), *e.g.* many of the ideas in fringe medicine appear to have *'leapt'* from **stage 1.1** to **stage 4.1.** Usually, the more stages an idea *'leaps'* the <u>less</u> sound it's likely to be, because it would not have been as rigorously tested. A *'leap'* takes place due to a sudden and unexpected public demand for that idea.

5) Falsification of an idea may not be enough to discredit it, especially when powerful parties have a vested interest in its maintenance and propagation (*e.g.* the disastrous official backing of fraudulent **Lysenko** genetics in **Stalinist Russia**). Conversely, verification may not actually guarantee the success of an idea, especially if it is <u>not</u> deemed as meeting practical needs or solving a problem as was the case with the voyages of discovery undertaken by China during the early fifteenth century. To gain social acceptance an idea <u>must be seen</u> to be of practical benefit.

6) Even widely accepted ideas can suddenly become discredited (or gradually eroded away) if they are falsified. This could happen through a new scientific discovery (*e.g.* the circulation of the blood by **William Harvey** in 1628) or negative publicity *e.g.* when **Aristotelian Cosmology** (a perspective long held by the **Roman Catholic Church** until well into the seventeenth century) was negated and replaced by an early modern **Cosmology.**

7) Some previously abandoned ideas may be revived (re-accepted) after having been temporarily discredited, (currently the case with **Nuclear Power**).

A diagrammatic representation of **The Longsight Pathway** is especially useful when tracing the progress of an idea (or belief) and is illustrated on the following page.

AN IDEA'S PROGRESSION IN PHASES AND STAGES

REASONS FOR AN IDEA'S FAILED DEVELOPMENT

Phase 1, Conception: Progression of an idea from a vague beginning to a peer group interest

1.1 Vague speculative *E.g.* Dark Energy
⇓

⇒ Incoherence

1.2 Coherent speculative *E.g.* Concept of a Multi-verse
⇓

⇒ Unverifiable

⇒ Lack of credibility

1.3 Peer group interest *e.g.* String Theory

Phase 2, Testing: Progression of an idea from a credible to a <u>narrow</u> peer group acceptance

2.1 Testable *E.g.* General Ether Theory
⇓

⇒ Falsification

2.2 Verified *E.g.* Quantum Theory
⇓

⇒ Complexity

2.3 Published *E.g.* Brown Dwarves
⇓

⇒ Limited readership

2.4 Formal Practical Confirmation *E.g.* Nuclear Fission
⇓

⇒ Official secrecy

2.5 Narrow, peer-group acceptance E.g. Dark Matter

⇒ Lack of obvious day-to-day relevance

Phase 3, Manufacture: Progression of an idea throughout design, manufacture and distribution

3.1 Designed Technology *E.g.* Nuclear Power
⇓

⇒ Folk panic

3.2 Mass Production *E.g.* Australian meat
⇓

⇒ Supply problems

3.3 Mass Distribution *E.g.* Typewriters

⇒ Obsolescence

Phase 4, Distribution: Progression of an idea through Society (some ideas may stop at **4.2**)

4.1 Consumer Demand *E.g.* Mobile Phones
⇓

⇒ Financial constraints

4.2 Wide Social Acceptance *E.g.* Belief in gravity
⇓

⇒ Complacency

4.3 Beleaguered Orthodoxy *E.g.* Miasma Theory
⇓

⇒ Defensiveness

4.4 Wide Social Rejection *E.g.* Aristotelian Cosmology
⇓

⇒ Available substitute

4.5 Revived Orthodoxy *E.g.* Nuclear Power again

⇒ Alternative replacement

Comments

The Longsight Pathway is that *'visual link'* between an idea's conception and its eventual acceptance within Society. However, what it does not show is <u>why</u> certain ideas successfully negotiate the *'pathway'* whilst others (equally as good) do not. **Gladwell (2004),** in his excellent book *'The Tipping Point,'* proffers one very good explanation. It shows that an idea, (*e.g.* fashion) reaches *'a tipping point'* where it gains acceptance within a given culture. However, this happens <u>only after the following criteria have been met</u>: -

1) The presence of a positive *'context'* – wherein a culture is already predisposed to accepting and absorbing the idea *e.g.* a widespread demand for better communications equipment.

2) The presence of an *'Innovator'* – who creates an idea and can solve any perceived problem, connected with it *e.g.* the ability to send information quickly. (The *'Innovator'* may have gathered knowledge of a positive context through prior research.)

3) The presence of a *'Connector'* – who recommends and spreads the idea through different sub-groups, *e.g.* a group of people sharing the same interests.

4) The presence of an *'Advocate'* – an expert who enthusiastically educates and informs influential people about the idea, *e.g.* a television academic.

5) The presence of a *'Salesman'* – who persuades (often large numbers) of people to embrace the idea. *'Salesmen'* often simplify the idea to communicate it more effectively amongst a wider public.

6) The presence of a *'Creative Imitator'* – who makes decisive small improvements to the original idea, moving it further away from failure and on toward success.

7) The presence of *'stickiness'* in an idea – causing it to remain within the public's mind and leading to its repeated use.

8) The presence of small groups (approximately **150** people) to test, adapt and promote the idea.

9) Miscellaneous contingency factors (or *'luck'*) which help promote the idea *e.g.* an *'Innovator'* might just *'happen'* to bump into a helpful *'Connector'* at a party.

The above criteria assume that enough resources exist to introduce and promote the idea. Should this not be the case then a *'Resource Provider'* will be needed. (This role could be discharged by a government or non-government organization, *e.g.* a *'Venture Capitalist'* or even by one's own friends and family) There needs to be enough financial and non-financial resources to successfully support an idea as it travels along the *'Pathway.'*

A vast promotional budget is <u>not</u> required for an idea to gain social acceptance. An expensive promotional campaign simply does not guarantee success – (<u>all</u> the above criteria are what is really needed). Conversely, as **Gladwell** has demonstrated, some ideas (those meeting <u>all</u> the above criteria) can spread like wildfire, even on a very a small budget. <u>He also implied that personal recommendation was the best means of promotion.</u>

The human element (the key people in **2-5**) represents the fundamental base upon which the other criteria **(6-9)** <u>must</u> build if the idea is to become wholly accepted. Each element is dependent upon the other – <u>all</u> of them must come into play.

Waller (2002) foreshadowed **Gladwell's** conclusions by suggesting that, within the specific area of scientific discovery, a radical idea gains widespread recognition when there is: -

- Perceived need for a creative breakthrough to resolve any major problem
- Good publicity and salesmanship on the part of those promoting the idea
- Opportunity, patronage and the resources to develop and publish the idea amongst influential parties
- Accuracy and professionalism amongst those promoting the idea
- Real and obvious practical benefits, which outdo those of any other substitute or competitor

As the debacle involving the **Piltdown Man Hoax** (during the last century) demonstrated, the presence of the first three preconditions may grant rapid and widespread acceptance of a false idea. However, the last two preconditions are needed – to discredit hoaxes and to enable the idea to retain a long-term acceptance. In contrast to religion and politics, the ideas which endure in modern science are those which are correct or where there's been an honesty and thoroughness on the part of the researchers promoting them. This is because the results of scientific mistakes tend to show up at a far earlier stage.

When an idea is falsified, it may go through a stage of beleaguered scientific orthodoxy (*e.g.* the dogged determination to cling to Ancient ways of thinking concerning the heart and blood vessels following the findings of **William Harvey**) before being finally abandoned. Alternatively, its abandonment may take place suddenly and without a struggle (as happened in the **1960s** with the theory of the **Steady State** Universe). Usually, when a widely-accepted idea is facing **anomalies** (soundly-based findings and facts that appear to contradict it) the situation arises wherein there's: -

- Shock and denial
- Increasingly desperate attempts to find fault with the findings
- Repeated attempts to modify the theory to account for the **anomalies**
- Reluctant abandonment of the old theory
- A convenient forgetfulness that the old theory had ever been followed with such fervor in the first place

Sources

Gladwell Malcolm (2004) *The Tipping Point: How Little Things Make a Big Difference,* Abacus ISBN: 0-349-11346-7

Hawkins Stephen (1988) *A Brief History of Time: From the Big Bang to Black Holes,* Bantam Books ISBN: 0-553-17521-1

Waller John (2002) *Fabulous Science: Fact and Fiction in the History of Scientific Discovery* Oxford University press ISBN: 0-192-80404-9

THE ROLE OF HUMAN RESOURCES IN WORKFORCE PLANNING

1. The role of Human Resources (HR) is best seen when contrasted with purely Personnel functions:

A Table Contrasting Human Resources with purely Personnel Functions

Human Resources	Personnel
Has a broad perspective which focuses upon the entire performance of an Organisation, especially the Financial, Marketing and Production areas	Has a narrow perspective, offering a specialised service that concentrates upon specific tasks within an Organisation e.g. processing wages
Assumes a volatile, changeable environment, creating a strong marketing orientation	Assumes a stable, rational environment, creating a strong inclination to behave in certain ways
Presupposes unpredictable career paths	Presupposes predictable career paths
Operates at the higher Managerial level. Corporate planning is central to its ethos	Operates at the junior Manager-Clerical level. Majors upon day-to-day operating decisions
Stresses expansion, *i.e.* how an Organisation may grow commercially and beat its competition whilst curbing Trade Union power	Stresses the maintenance of Organisational status. Wishes to maintain good relations with Trade Unions
Seeks to forecast trends by closely monitoring the environment. Is mainly outward-looking	Seeks to handle employee related problems and is mainly inward-looking
Emphasises the need for: - • Core competences • A *'leading edge'* over competitors • High performance in every area • Strictly controlled finance • *'Total quality'* in production • Managerial effectiveness • A positive sense of mission and philosophy • Systematic analyses and forecasts	Emphasises the need for: - • Organisational development • Work-Force Planning • Systematic training • Job enrichment and appraisal • Salary administration • Managerial paternalism • Good industrial relations • Legal knowledge
Important in status, playing a major role in strategic planning and policy implementation – has become dominant since the mid 1980s	Marginalized in status and virtually absorbed within the Human Resources Field – was prevalent during the 1950s to early 1980s

2. Without repeating all the above information, Human Resources relates to Work Force Planning by: -

a) Establishing and firmly embedding the basic ethos, mission and philosophy of an Organisation. This is of importance when seeking to influence both internal and external customers

b) Carefully monitoring the external business environment by collecting valid and reliable data

c) Assessing all the Human Resources within the Organisation (alongside the other resources like financial capital needed for its smooth functioning). Performing both internal and external audits whenever necessary

d) Considering all the available options which could help the Organisation relate effectively to its *'shop floor'* and wider business environment

e) Encouraging definite Policy decisions, *i.e.* whether to offer higher wages, recruit a different type of staff, shed labour or review interviewing procedures

f) Prompting the development of *'feedback loops'* which determine the validity of Policy decisions

3. Human Resource and Personnel Departments have a mix of roles that are constantly changing as time progresses. The dominance of **ICT** has had a continuing long-term effect upon these roles by requiring the continued learning of new skills and work practices within the workplace.

Additional Note: The Levels of Plagiarism

Legal Disclaimer: *This is an introductory guide to the main issues surrounding Plagiarism and the disciplinary measures which may result from it. The author disclaims responsibility for any unfavourable outcome readers of this information may incur in relation to Plagiarism and other related issues. None of the following information is meant to be a substitute for professional advice and guidance.*

A **quote** is a copying of words from a source and enclosing them within double quotation marks.
A **citation** is a reporting of what a source stated (and has no quotation marks). It involves altering the words of a source but not its meaning. Achieving this requires a good command of the English language.
All quotations and citations must be fully referenced, *i.e.* having the name/s of the author/s attached to them and the year (or month and year) of publication. This can be done with (or without) the aid of brackets, *e.g.* **Richard Smith (2013) suggested** or **Per one suggestion (R. Smith 2013).**

In general, Educational Institutions recognize the following three levels of Plagiarism:
Level 1: When a quote has been used as a citation – even though the source was properly referenced.
Level 2: When material from a source has been used without acknowledgement.
Level 3: When an attempt has been made to put forward a whole body of work as one's own. (This explains why a *'third party'* i.e. a friend, colleague or even a Private Tutor should NEVER act a *'Ghost Writer'* (which means doing the student's work for them). Attempting to do this would *'aid and abet'* **Level 3** Plagiarism. If detected it would cause irreparable damage to the professional reputation and personal integrity of all concerned. (A *'ghost writer's'* style is rarely the same as that of the original; it would *'read differently'* and so be easily detected, especially with the aid of current technology.)

Level 2 and **Level 3** Plagiarism are self-explanatory, incurring such penalties as cancellation of a degree and even expulsion from the Institution concerned. However, confusion often surrounds **Level 1** due to: -
- Uncertainty over whether Plagiarism has taken place at all
- Inadequate training of the student who has been left insufficiently informed about it
- Intermittent and haphazard bouts of reinforcement by Educational Institutions who, at times, appear to ignore it altogether

Level 1 Plagiarism is the use of a quote as a citation. An Academic Department may decide that a quote has been used as a citation even when one or two words from the original have been altered and the source properly referenced. However, it must be stressed that a quote only becomes a citation following a **substantial alteration in wording** with no alteration in meaning. To change a quote into a citation requires a good command of the English language – which many overseas students find challenging. The easier (but incorrect) option is to alter only a few words of the original quote – hoping this will suffice to change it into a citation. Doing this pushes the work dangerously close to **Level 1** Plagiarism (with its subsequent disciplinary measures *i.e.* a loss of marks). Another bad alternative is to over-use quotations - the student often finding it easier to recall a whole quote rather than laboriously changing it into a citation. This results in lost marks due to *'filling out'* the work with too many quotes!

Generally, undergraduates are authorised to quote up to fifteen words (taken from each individual source); a postgraduate thesis can quote up to forty words and a writer of books one hundred and twenty words. These rules apply if the source isn't a song or a poem (in which case substantial payment may be requested before a *'right to use'* is granted. However, titles of songs and poems may be quoted.) Sometimes an Educational Institution may be given the right to replicate up to 5% of a text book. This can only be done by qualified staff (not students) for teaching purposes and on a *'not for profit'* basis.

Another unhelpful complication regarding Plagiarism stems from the Academic Institutions themselves. Many of them overlook the fact that some of their overseas students have only a limited grasp of English – particularly *'legalistic'* English. Sadly (and all too often) these students are simply directed to a Departmental Web Site to locate the necessary information on Plagiarism. However, the information found is often expressed in such legalistic jargon that it requires a postgraduate degree in English and Law to even begin to understand it! The unhappy result is genuine confusion and bewilderment on the part of the student, leading to inadvertent **Level 1** Plagiarism.

Matters are not helped when Departments appear (often for years gone by) to have done very little about Plagiarism and then, in a fit of self-righteousness, arbitrarily clamp down upon students who may be in the second or third year of their degree. At the very least students may lose vital marks and at worst their personal integrity will have been called into question. In such situations, it's nearly always the student and rarely the Department that's held to blame. Such unfair *'scapegoating'* can be especially prominent at *'Departmental Hearings'* (which often have all the fairness of a Stalinist *'Show Trial'*). Any protest from the student is met with the stock phrase, *'You should have referred to the regulations found on our website.'* (Conveniently omitted is the fact that these regulations are often expressed in incomprehensible legalistic jargon.) Departmental Staff will wish to protect their own reputation and so place the blame squarely upon the student – who may even be accused of being *'difficult'* or *'uncooperative.'*

What can the poor student do when they face an accusation of **Level 1** Plagiarism? Preferably, before this stage has been reached (and their reputation jeopardised) he/she needs to have taken the following steps – either individually or along with other similarly-placed students: -
Step 1: To have obtained written (or email) confirmation of the Department's Policy in relation to Plagiarism. Should the Policy have been expressed in an incomprehensible form of English then the student must point this out and request a simpler written explanation
Step 2: To have hired a reputable translator to express the Policy's terms in a language which can be understood. (Beware – great care must be taken – some translators may possess little or no legal expertise)
Step 3: To have studied helpful resources like the *'Writers & Artists Year Handbook'* which explains legal matters in a very concise and user-friendly way. (Such resources are available in Academic and most Public Libraries or from www.writersandartists.co.uk.)
Step 4: To have obtained legal advice (preferably with the aid of the Students' Union)
Steps 2-3 need to be carefully considered should **Step 1** have had an unsatisfactory outcome. **Step 4** will almost certainly be needed should there be a serious dispute within a Department.

Departments could greatly help matters if they made it mandatory that students attend an *'Induction session on Plagiarism'* (chaired by the Head of Department to lend added authority). Each student attendee should understand that no marks will be awarded (at all) until they have signed an attendance form to confirm their presence at such a session. Departments could also provide translators to ensure that students for whom English is a second language can gain a firm grasp of the relevant regulations. Once the above support has been given it should then be made very clear that responsibility for breaching these regulations will henceforth lie firmly with the student. A Contract regarding Plagiarism should be drawn up and signed (by both the student and Department concerned) stating that the student has understood and accepted all its guidelines.

However, budgetary constraints often mean that Departments are rarely able to adopt such sensible measures. Students are simply left alone with the (often unhelpful) web site to *'get it right'* about Plagiarism. The wisest option is to resolve this issue at the earliest opportunity *i.e.* at the very beginning of a course. It should never be left unresolved only to produce a crisis later. This means that it must be done early, with the Department in question before a dispute arises. Preventing allegations of Plagiarism from ever happening is by far the better option.

BIBLIOGRAPHY

Barras Robert (1982)   *Students Must Write:*   ISBN: 0-416-33620-5 (Pbk)
A guide to better writing in   Ref. 378.1 Bar
casework and examinations
Methuen & Co Ltd

Barras Robert (1984)   *Study!*   ISBN: 0-412-25690-8 (Pbk)
A guide to effective study,   Ref. 378.4
revision and examination
techniques
Chapman and Hall Ltd

Cassie Fisher W. &   *Student's Guide to Success*   ISBN: 0-333-23277-1 (Pbk)
Constantine T. (1977)   MacMillan Press Ltd   Ref. 378.1 Cas

Freeman Richard (1991)   *Mastering Study Skills*   ISBN: 0-333-54929-5 (Pbk)
Macmillan Press Ltd   Ref. 378.1 Fre

Lengefeld Uelaine (1987)   *Study Skill Strategies*   ISBN: 1-85091-737-X (Pbk)
How to learn more in less time   Ref. 378.1 Len
Crisp Publications Inc

Marshall A. Lorraine &   *A Guide to Learning*   ISBN: 0-335-10117-8
Francis Rowland (1983)   *Independently*   Ref. 378.1 Mar
Open University Press

Northedge Andrew (1991)   *The Good Study Guide*   ISBN: 0-7492-0048
Open University   Ref. 378.1

Palmer Richard &   *Brain Training:*   ISBN: 0-419-13110-8 (Pbk)
Pope Chris (1984)   *Studying for success*   Ref. 378.1 Pal
E and F, N. Spon Ltd

Rowntree Derek (1980)   *Learn How to Study*   ISBN: 0-354-4009-X
MacDonald General Books   Ref. 378.1 Row

Williams Kate (1989)   *Study Skills:*   ISBN: 0-333-48694-3 (Hbk)
A Programmed Introduction to   Ref. 378.1 Wil
Better Study Techniques
Macmillan Educational

For up to date legal information on such issues as Copyright, Libel and Plagiarism please refer to the latest available edition of either *'The Writer's Yearbook,'* (published by A & C Black) or *'The Writer's Handbook'* (published by Macmillan Reference Books). Copies should be available in most Public Libraries. Up to date information on Study Techniques can be found on the Internet, examples of which are given on the next page.

'Advantage Study Skills' is a very useful general introduction to the *'Palgrave Study Skills Books'* and to *'Smarter Study Skills'* series produced by Pearson Educational Publishers. Those offer a more detailed exploration of some of the topics covered in this manual. Either place the above names in a good search engine or just visit any University bookshop.

For further information please visit www.rjs-tutor.co.uk

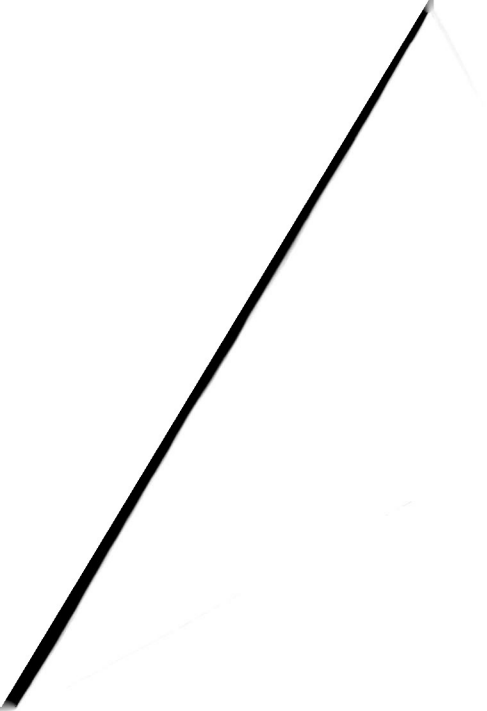

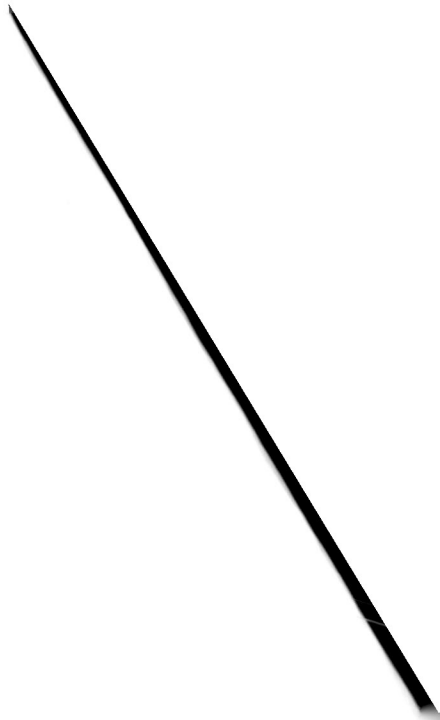